Fifteen Pauses

The life-changing silence and stillness of Japanese Ma

Tom Frengos

First published in 2024 by Tom Frengos
Copyright © 2024 Tom Frengos

The contents of this document are protected by copyright, except where it is referenced to another author or publication. No part of this material may be reproduced by any process, electronic or otherwise, in any material form, or transmitted to any other person or stored electronically in any form without prior permission of the author.

Tom Frengos asserts the moral right to be identified as the author of this work.

Typeset by Romina Cavagnola, Alchemy of Alignment™ Publishing
Cover design and illustrations by Kumiko Albee
Infographics by Tom Frengos
Calligraphy characters designed by Tomoko Abe and Tom Frengos

Printed and bound globally by Lightning Source using sustainable resources.

First edition
Paperback: 978-4-9913679-0-8
eBook: 978-4-9913679-1-5

For my dear brother George

and my beloved wife Mariko

Contents

Contents..i
Acknowledgements..iii
Who is this book for?..iv

PART I: MA – DISCOVERING A NEW WAY OF LIVING
Prologue: One word out of nothing....................................1
Chapter 1: Ma is in everything we do.................................5
Chapter 2: Space is sacred and meaningful.....................20

PART II: OUR MENTAL, EMOTIONAL AND SOCIAL PAUSES
Chapter 3: Change is an eternal dance.............................41
Chapter 4: *Mikansei* – incompleteness is beautiful.......58
Chapter 5: Emptiness means possibility..........................74
Chapter 6: Pause and read the air.....................................98
Chapter 7: *Maai* – create a graceful space....................120
Chapter 8: Open your space for change.........................147

PART III: EXISTENTIAL PAUSES – WHO AM I BECOMING?
Chapter 9: Be friends with the void................................163
Chapter 10: *Michiyuki* – journey in stillness................177
Chapter 11: *Suki Ma* – take a deep breath....................200

Chapter 12: Surrender to the pause.................................219
Chapter 13: Who am I becoming?.....................................239

PART IV: PAUSING AT OUR ARRIVAL
Chapter 14: *Susumu* – move forward..............................265
Epilogue: *Yoin* – the long goodbye..................................273

EXTRA RESOURCES
Glossary of terms...281
References..289
About the author: Tom Frengos...304

Acknowledgements

I would like to thank my mentor, Adam, who planted the seeds for this book. My friends Paul, Lisa, Adriana, Ian and Deborah and George have also been important in giving me honest feedback that helped me grow as a writer and as a person. Special acknowledgments to my calligraphy and Japanese teachers, and Kumiko who designed this book cover and designed the illustrations. Her work embodies the spirit of Ma.

This book wouldn't be possible without the fantastic editing work from my editor Lu and the encouragement from my sister Tricia. I would also like to thank my brother George who helped me see that the joy in writing is not in the accolades but rather the work, the endless hours of typing and revising. Writing is a journey that shouldn't be rushed but rather enjoyed. Finally, I would like to give a special thank you to my wife Mariko who taught me everything about Japanese culture and how I came to love this culture as much as she did.

My brother George and my wife Mariko never got to see this book published but I can honestly say their voices, their hearts and spirits are forever intertwined in every page, every graphic, every word of this book. This book is my love letter to them.

Who is this book for?

Can you sit patiently in silence? Do you wish you had more time for yourself, more spaces in your life to stop and rest?

The fact that you are reading this book suggests to me that you have thought about making changes to your life. Perhaps you are thinking there must be a new life out there for you, a life you have overlooked, even undervalued in the past but are now considering – a life where success and well-being isn't solely measured by how much we achieve, how busy we are, or how fast we get things done.

Fifteen Pauses offers that alternative life. It is built on the Japanese philosophy of Ma – a space and time to pause in silence, emptiness and stillness. If you live and work in Japan, have friends, or partners who are Japanese you may have even heard about Ma or experienced it. Even if you have, this book will help you better understand the deeper layers of Japanese culture, and discover a better way of living.

Ma is based on our human need to rest and reset, to transform within a pause. Fifteen Pauses explains how staying in moments of silence, emptiness, stillness is a pathway to change. Mastering these pauses strengthens our resolve, summons up our courage to weather the stormy transitions we all face in our lives.

This book is suitable for coaches, psychologists, counsellors, teachers – anyone who believes that the pause is a superpower that needs to be shared with the world. This book is intended to create a revolution, to transform our view of a pause – to remind us that a pause doesn't mean failure, a lack of confidence or a lack of ambition. A pause is the missing piece we all need to become better human beings.

PART I:
Ma – Discovering a new way of living

PROLOGUE:
One word out of nothing

> *If you give people nothingness,*
> *they can ponder what can be achieved*
> *from that nothingness.*
> **– Tadao Ando**
> **Japanese architect**

This book was born in the most unlikely place – in a counseling session talking about nothing.

I remember that day clearly, sitting anxiously in that session almost 14 years ago. I was talking to my psychologist about the full life I was leading: my non-stop work, my sleepless nights, the lack of free space in my life. I leaned forward in my seat as I talked about the anxiety that followed me everywhere – while teaching, while socializing with friends, while on planes. I remember telling him that all those relaxation exercises, the deep breathing, the mindfulness that managed this anxiety were no longer working. The harder I tried to fight these feelings off, the harder they stuck to me.

Finished, and feeling disappointed, I sank back into my chair, feeling helpless, remaining silent, my arms now open and waiting for an answer. There were a dozen seconds of silence that followed, annoying silence I recall. I looked to my psychologist, expecting him to give me a few words of empathy like *it must be hard* or *it will pass and get easier*, but no words came. I waited for some solutions from him, something I hoped would take away these feelings. Instead, I got more silence.

I remember that day, my shoulders dropping in defeat, leaning back in my seat, looking up as I cursed, "I wish these feelings would f#$k off."

Still no words from him. No sigh. No clearing of the throat. Just silence.

"So, what do I do?"

More silence.

My psychologist moved in his seat. He folded his arms, brought his two knuckles up to rest on the bottom of his chin. He seemed ready to speak, ready to give me advice I thought. I felt a glimmer of hope.

He said, "Nothing."

Did I hear him right? How can I do nothing? I paid him this much to tell me to do nothing?

I asked again with a doubtful look. "Nothing? Seriously?"

Smiling, he leaned back into his chair, then repeated in a confident and reassuring tone, "Do nothing."

I fully didn't understand what he meant in that session, but as I reflected on it that week, two very important messages came to mind. First, I should stop fighting these feelings and embrace them. The second, perhaps the most important message from him – pause.

I can confidently say that one word started my journey – a journey where I discovered, when the moment is right, doing nothing can be life-changing.

***

On March 23rd, 2020, I discovered that doing nothing is difficult, especially when sitting in an uncomfortable seat, on a long-haul flight to Tokyo.

It's reasonable to assume that some of us find long haul flights uncomfortable. Some of you reading this might even not like planes. Being confined in a tin tube flying over 11,000 meters doesn't seem all that fun I was thinking. Inside you have no control over when you arrive. You are in limbo, stuck between where you were and where you want to be.

How do we occupy this limbo time? We watch movies, eat, drink, read, sleep, listen to music, prepare for a meeting, move around the cabin, even complain. Sitting on a plane and doing nothing is not an option. We need to do something.

Eight hours into the flight, I finished my third movie but there were no other movies I wanted to see. We still had four hours. I then started thinking about the mess our world was in. I thought I should try some meditation to erase these busy thoughts torturing my weary mind. It had worked for me before. Hopefully it could work again. I hoped to forget what was happening in the world. I needed a mental oasis, somewhere in the present to briefly escape from an uncertain and bleak looking future. I needed to think of nothing.

I turned off my entertainment screen, and sat back in what now seemed to be a plush couch that I happily sank myself into. I put my restless hands on my unsteady lap, then focused my eyes on the screen in the distance and locked my gaze on it. Being still agitated me, but soon I settled into this pose, being still, doing nothing for nearly an hour.

Not long after the cabin brightened. I looked to my left, through the half open window shade. The setting sun peaked through the auburn-coloured clouds. Orange and yellow rays entered the dimly lit cabin and rested on my now steady hands. One Japanese word popped into my mind. Amazingly, it explained what I needed, what the world needed.

It was **Ma**.

CHAPTER 1:
Ma is in everything we do

Ma is a key to Japanese. Not only in architecture, but in daily life, art, music – every moment, every kind of behavior.
– Arata Isozaki
Japanese architect

If anyone needed a book about Ma, it would be me.

At the best of times, I can be caring, calm, even a good listener if you can believe that. At my worst, I am restless, impatient, even annoying. Until I reached my 50s, my life could be best described as someone who was always in a hurry to get things done. I was rushing to a finish line with everyone else around me screaming at me to slow down.

I am not sure whether this had to do with how stressed I was, how busy I was, the type of work I did, or even my personality, but for whatever reason, I saw little value in a long pause. The idea of sitting still, waiting to reach the front of a long queue, remaining locked in a meditative pose in a dark room while trying to think of nothing – none of this was fun at all. I was sure that many people would have agreed with me that a long pause is unnatural.

When I moved to Japan in 2017 and discovered the Japanese word Ma in a bookstore, my view of the pause changed. I knew then if I wanted better relationships, greater well-being, a better life, I needed to make peace with the pause.

In short, I needed more Ma.

***

Ma is a Japanese word for a pause, a gap, a silence, a sense of timing, an interval between events, a time and space between where we were and where we want to be. Many of my fellow expatriates in Japan were fascinated by this concept when I told them about it, but I sensed few of them, if any, could fully appreciate how living it could transform our lives.

I was instinctively drawn to this concept because it seemed poetic, and relevant to my work, but I would have to say it was mostly because I needed more pauses. This concept appealed to me on a personal, professional and spiritual level – so much that it encouraged me to keep reading. It awakened in me a passion, some might even say an obsession, to build on the brilliant work of poets, architects, filmmakers, academics and artists.

Despite my efforts to unveil some of its mystery, this Japanese concept remained mysterious, ambiguous, even frustrating for me. With so many meanings, I struggled to give a 15-second elevator pitch about it to friends, family, literary agents and prospective clients. I spent 2 years asking Japanese business people and academics about it. I even presented this concept at a Tokyo conference. In this 2-year journey, I was vainly hoping that this elevator pitch would magically materialize when I needed it – but it never did.

In 2020, it was becoming clearer to me that Ma isn't just something we talk about, write about or debate over. It must also be experienced, felt and lived. As I began practicing it and living it, my elevator pitch was gaining form. Ma seemed more like a way of life that Japanese people rarely speak about, yet eloquently express in their bows, patience, grace, and silence. It is an invisible thread carefully and lovingly interwoven into the fabric of Japanese society, an eternal bond that unites all living and non-living things as a single entity, a precious Japanese philosophy longing to be discovered and shared with the world.

After 3 years, I discovered the secret power of this philosophy; I now truly believed that if we added more pauses to our lives, we would have greater well-being, better relationships, more innovation, more personal meaning. We could transform our lives, navigate through life transitions.

In March 2020, the world paused. On that plane bound for Tokyo, as the sunlight entered the cabin, I wondered who we could become in this pause or any pause.

So what is Ma really about? What can it teach us about the pause? How can a pause enrich our lives?

A BITTERSWEET PAUSE

Ma is a pause in everyday life. It is a long red traffic light, a traffic jam, a time and space where we must wait, even though we want life to keep moving along. Pauses like these are bitter, annoying, probably because many of us believe that a pause is uncomfortable, especially when it is longer than normal and we are unsure as to when it will end. Some of us might think a pause stops us from achieving, doing things, living our lives. For some of us, these long waits can evoke feelings of non-being and nothingness, a blank space that distorts our sense of time, creating the illusion that we have been waiting forever.

A long pause can mean discomfort, even tension. But as we sit longer in this tension, and hold our urge to leave it, we achieve a breakthrough – a transformation. We discover a pause doesn't mean we are doing nothing or giving up something. It actually means we are gaining something. We realize that pausing our actions, our voice, our judgments can open up new worlds for us. It slows life down. It turns off the noise. It gives us what we desperately need in a busy life.

Pausing gives us the patience to wait in that emptiness and nothingness; it dissolves the illusions and falsehoods we hear, see and feel when we begin our pause. A pause allows the light of truth to slowly emerge out of this anxious wait. Ma is the bittersweet pause we all need in our lives.

UNCOMFORTABLE, LIBERATING SILENCE

These bittersweet pauses are found in silent moments. They evoke uncomfortable anxieties, uncertainty, even doubt within us. When there is silence between us, we may assume the worst – that something is wrong with our relationships or even with us. We think we are being silenced, stopped from expressing our views, stopped from being promoted, stopped from achieving our potential, stopped from living our lives. In silence, we feel out of control and an unbearable longing to break that silence.

Silence is also liberating. We feel this as we quietly walk through an empty field that stretches for miles, with no tree, no mountain, no city, no house, no other person in sight. We feel scared in this silence and emptiness but at the same time we also feel a freedom. We sense a chance to reset and discover a strength that keeps us going.

Silence awakens the emotions we have kept buried for so long. We feel beautiful tension in silence when a musician pauses their music. At first, we wonder when the music will return and what the musician will do next. We even guess what will happen next. Remaining in this silence frees us from our own worlds, places us in a time and space where we understand the musician in silence, where words aren't needed and where we, in a brief crack in time, share one heart and one mind.

A CRACK WHERE LIGHT SHINES

Silence creates cracks in space and time, rest areas along the superhighway of life that appear out of nowhere. We can find them in a quiet park, a tree for us to lean against, a stairwell in our office to catch our breath, a free moment for us to text our loved ones, or even a long pause we need to gather our thoughts before we speak. These cracks are private, safe spaces to remind us who we really are, to ask ourselves what we want out of life, and to embrace what life is offering us now. A crack is our personal sanctuary where our dreams have a voice, a hopeful space where we wait for our faith to be rewarded. We need patience and awareness to find these cracks, and a time and desire to enter and stay in them. If we stay in them long enough, they give us the light to move forward in the darkness.

THE SPEAKING WHITE SPACE

The distance between boundaries, objects, living things and people is also Ma – the physical space we share, the rules around how far and how close we stand, work and live from each other. It is the white space we need to keep our distance, to break away from the endless chatter, to shut out the BS from our lives. It is where we establish our safe space, declutter our lives, and cast out the toxic energy and people we want out of our lives forever.

These white spaces exist in a painting, a book or even an empty room of a home we have just moved into. It is an empty sea of nothingness, beautiful nothingness – a void that communicates with us, works with us to imagine an alternative future, hopefully a better one.

A RELATIONSHIP BAROMETER

Our relationships and well-being depend on our ability to notice and create more of these whitespaces, our ability to read the physical and psychological distance between us, our ability to analyse the feelings and mood in the spaces we share. Ma is a barometer that reads this distance between us, our actions, our pauses, our silence, our hidden thoughts. It determines whether the space between us, the Ma, is good or bad.

When it is good, we are in sync with each other, like a singer who instinctively raises her voice as the guitarist changes a chord. It happens when we work together as a team, when we are in harmony with nature, and aren't trying to control it or exploit it. It is peaceful coexistence where we are letting people shine, allowing each other to speak uninterrupted, and we aren't judging them.

The space we share can also be bad. It happens when we fight for space, strongly disagree, interrupt and talk over each other, and refuse to listen. It is being out of rhythm, not coexisting, and not acting as a team. It is an unhealthy, uncomfortable, toxic space where we feel anxious, confused, breathless, inauthentic. We want to run away from these bad spaces.

BEING IN THE 'NOW' SPACES

Ma is a liminal in-between 'now' space: the daily journey from point A to point B, a train commute to work, a drive to a destination, a transition point between our private lives and our work lives. It is a career change, being in between jobs, an anxious, hopeful wait for our visa application to be approved.

This space can be uncomfortable, especially when point A and B are more attractive. In this space, we either worry about what we left behind or worry about a future that has not yet arrived. We want to live in the past to remember the good times. We want to rush to the end, to get to work on time, to get our visa application approved, to get a new job, to secure that gold medal. When we hold this space, we focus on the here and now, what we can control in the present. We come to appreciate this 'now' space for it is unique, fleeting and can't be revisited.

HOPEFUL AND UNCERTAIN SPACES

In these 'now' spaces, we learn to pause and notice our mixed feelings about starting a new job, a new school, even a new journey. We feel hopeful that we can make this new experience whatever we want it to be, that everything will work out. Yet we also are scared and apprehensive, unsure of how things are going to turn out. We worry if we will get along with each other. We wonder if anything good will come out of this, whether we will succeed. In the face of this doubt, we begin the journey.

JOURNEY OF COURAGE AND HOPE

Japanese architects like Kengo Kuma and space and well-being architects like Yoko Kawai believe that Ma is also a journey, an unchartered territory, an uncertain future we travel towards, with no clear end in sight. I like to think that in this journey, we bravely leave our old world behind, sail through a shoreless sea with no past to anchor us in. In this journey, we fear that we may not reach our destination but, at the same time, we have faith that we will reach that shore. We sense a distant shore hidden behind the clouds, a storm, and the vast sea; we feel an energizing hope that the storm will fade; we believe the clouds will lift and a new world will appear.

A TIME AND SPACE OF BECOMING

Ma consists of two Japanese *kanji* characters that come from the Chinese language. The first one means *mon* or gate while the second one, placed between those gates is *hi* (pronounced hee) which means sun or day. When I stopped to look at how Ma is written and these characters, I discovered a poetic, rather deeper meaning behind it, and more importantly, the transformational potential behind a pause.

間 - *ma* or pause, silence, a gap
門 - *mon* or gate
日 - *hi* (pronounced hee) - sun/day

Japanese and international writers, poets, academics, artists believe the mon gates represent borders, people, the beginning and end of a conversation, a project, a movie, a journey. The hi character in the middle means sun or metaphorically the light of change that shines through the gates. It is here where something is happening between these gates, the silence, the stop in action, the pause in our lives.

PAUSING BETWEEN THE GATES

When we pause between these gates, we sense rebirth; we notice a change of light, smell, temperature in a room; we recall something from our past that can haunt us, and inspire us. In this journey, unfinished ideas become finished, conversations resume, understanding unfolds, relationships grow, discoveries are made, new dreams begin. Ma is a journey of pauses and waiting for something, and ourselves, to become better.

THE LIGHT COMING THROUGH THE GATES

FIFTEEN PAUSES

Fifteen Pauses is a journey to becoming better friends, partners, leaders, colleagues, human beings. Each pause represents the fleeting poetic union between the human joys and anxieties in holding a pause, and the life changing transformations that emerge within it. These pauses are restorative breaks from a busy world we all secretly crave – safe spaces to listen, dream, cry, play, rest. They are thresholds to a new reality, a chance to learn new things, change our habits, see the world through a clearer lens. Fifteen Pauses is living the life we always wanted and becoming the person we dreamed of being.

This book is divided into four parts. Part I introduces Ma as a new way of life – a life where we pause to appreciate the present moment, a life to discover our sacred spaces and their power to inspire us. Part II focuses on our mental and emotional pauses, the long pauses that make us uncomfortable, the ones that awaken our human need to fill these pauses with our judgments, our anxieties, our fears. These chapters explain how letting our thoughts pass us by, giving our emotional reactions time to settle down can strengthen us, free us. In chapters 3, 4 and 5 we will learn why we should hold the silence and emptiness, why we need more white spaces in our lives, why the process is a necessary pathway to perfection, and why we should wait in a pause even when we think nothing is happening. The remaining three chapters focus on our social pauses. Chapters 6 and 7 explain how we read others in the space we share in work, play, silence and inaction. It reminds us how stopping to gauge that space, observing the silence and distance between us, is the key to maintaining and growing healthy relationships with people and with nature. Chapter 8 talks about opening the space for others to talk, to share, to co-create with us, to create better stories between us. Opening the space is a willingness to pause and bravely open our own hearts and to patiently wait for another person to open theirs.

Part III focuses on the existential pauses we take to becoming a new person. Chapter 9 explains how periods of transition like the loss of a loved one, a career change evokes feelings of loneliness, emptiness and loss, and how embracing these feelings strengthens our resilience, expresses our creativity. Chapters 10, 11 and 12 explain that Ma is also our unique journey, and why we should never look too far ahead and why we should never rush to the end. In our journeys, the pauses, the waits, the reflections, the uncertainties and fears we confront – all of these transform the situation and ourselves. Chapter 13 reminds us to enjoy the journey of becoming someone new rather than rushing to our arrival.

Part IV embodies the two short pauses we need to reach our arrival. In Chapter 14, we discover how moving closer to our goal excites us; how it makes hesitate to move forward; and how we might need a short pause before we let go, and move deeper towards our new beginning. The epilogue, "*Yoin*: the long good-bye," is the final look back to celebrate what we have achieved; to remember what we have lost; to fondly remember what we have learned and who we have become in these pauses.

GETTING THE MOST OUT OF THIS BOOK

This book became my personal guide on how to live through the *Great Pause* and how we can live beyond it. Yet, in writing about this and living this life, I now know that we don't need to be in a global pause to use Ma. Nor do we have to be Japanese or living in Japan. A pause is a human ideal that we can all recognize and all need. We can all use it anytime and anywhere.

To get the most out of this book, I recommending writing down what you have learned from each chapter. Think of how you can apply these pauses to your everyday life. After that, go out into the world and practice these new behaviours. In this journey, you will have successes. You will also have setbacks. Try your best to remain determined, even if you don't master these new behaviours right away. You will learn from these setbacks, and, from them, you will fine tune your new skills so that they become second nature.

A kind reminder: our journeys will be different. We may all walk the same path, read the same chapters, say the same things, but each of us will add our own stories to make this book more personally meaningful to us. We will face and overcome our own roadblocks, make our own discoveries as we start pausing more.

Join me on this journey to unlocking the secret powers of the Fifteen Pauses.

CHAPTER 2:

Space is sacred and meaningful

Space has the power to improve your well-being – we tend to forget that.
– Dr. Yoko Kawai
Architect, space and wellness designer,
Yale University professor

When people ask me what places in Tokyo I miss the most, I immediately say it wasn't a place but a space, a table in a Tokyo coffee shop that I missed the most. Every time I arrived in Tokyo from Fukuoka, I would head straight to this coffee shop located in Tokyo station. I often arrived around 2pm, which was a quiet time so I could choose wherever I wanted to sit, but it was this table in front of the coffee machine, facing the deli and the wine section, that I fondly remembered in late 2020.

The last time I visited this shop was in January 2020. I remember blissfully savoring my cappuccino, soaking in the sound of the coffee machine releasing steam as the barista prepared a coffee for a very impatient customer. I gratefully breathed in the bitter coffee aroma as the barista slowly and calmly poured the coffee into the cup with artistic precision while the customer tapped his anxious hands on the counter.

From my favourite space, I happily watched commuters hurrying in an anxious state through the jam-packed Tokyo station. I turned my attention back to the store and watched customers milling around the sweet section. Some customers were putting sweets into their baskets while others were reluctantly returning them to their place on the shelves. I smiled as I watched the customers behind me leisurely checking out the assorted pastas and olive oils at the back of the store.

For two years that space on the table was my entry portal into Tokyo. Going there was a ritual that prepared me for my work. At this table I meticulously planned my training sessions, playing out scenarios in my head for how they would run. In this space, I also chatted away with the very friendly staff, talking about the recent sumo wrestling results, the places I can visit and eat at in Tokyo. I remember the baristas carving a nice character or writing into the milky froth of my cappuccino. In October, I got a pumpkin. In December, I got either a snowman or a Santa. I happily accepted whatever I got in this space, for it was where I felt the most at peace.

I couldn't be in this space right now, but I could vividly recall the marble-like texture of that table, the uplifting smells of coffee, the freshly toasted focaccia, and the soft jazz music harmoniously mixing in with the coffee machine in action. When I stopped to think of this space in 2020, it became clearer to me just how important space is to us all. The spaces we live and work in are reservoirs of memories. They comfort us and inspire us when we need them the most – even when we aren't physically there.

JAPANESE CONCEPT OF SPACE AND TIME

It's difficult to grasp Ma without understanding the Japanese concept of space, particularly why it's important to pause and treasure these spaces we live and work in. Space is important in Japan because there isn't much of it. Approximately 70% of Japan is covered by forest, meaning 30% of Japan's area houses most of the 126.05 million (as estimated by Worldometer in 2020) people living on this island nation.

Japan is 1/20th the size of Australia and yet has 5 times more people. At the time of writing, Japan was ranked the 10th largest population in the world. Given the limited amount of space in Japan, it is easy to understand why space is respected by Japanese people – almost worshipped. We can see that 'worship' expressed in their daily lives, their architecture, their Shintō and Zen Buddhism religion. In Japan, space must be respected, admired, valued, shared with our neighbours, colleagues and fellow citizens in harmony. Think of how uncomfortable it would be if people were fighting with each other in that small space.

SPACE IS SUBJECTIVE AND TRANSIENT

Ma is tied into the concept of space, but it isn't as simple as it sounds. Space is transient, nonphysical, subjective and time related. It is the last time we spoke and when we resume our conversation. It is bravely stepping out of the limelight without the fear of losing it. It is taking a one-year sabbatical to travel the world, or creating space between ourselves and our significant others to reflect. Remember your love interest telling you that he/she needed some space? Space is somewhere we pause to think things over before acting, whether we keep the relationship going or whether we give them the flick.

Space is subjective. It is we who put the meaning in that space, not others. A space in a tucked away corner of an office can mean freedom and privacy for one person. It can mean power for a manager. It can mean exclusion for someone else. It is an interpretation, a feeling of how much space we need. We move forward to show closeness and then retreat two steps backward from a heated conversation. We take a step back to regain perspective and to feel safe. When there are no physical boundaries or borders, even moving a few feet away from a threat can give us that safety.

The key thing to remember is that spaces also change in form and in meaning over time as we silently sit still in them and move through them. They can become spiritual as the light enters the room, become sacred as we pass through a gate on the way to a shrine. Ma is the magic and change of a space in time.

SPACE MEANS POWER AND SUCCESS

Space is something we fight over. The more of it we have, the more powerful we feel and become. The more power we have, the more we dominate a conversation, the more our shadow dominates the space, the more difficult it is for other people to claim their own.

Space can define power and hierarchy. In the Japanese workplace, and to lesser degree in other cultures, lower ranked employees have less space than higher ranked employees. CEOs or owners of an organization usually sit at the back of the office. This comes from an age-old wisdom that a person in power shouldn't be easily accessible, especially if there are enemies trying to get him or her.

MAINTAIN YOUR PERSONAL BOUNDARIES

Our personal boundaries represent the optimal distance we keep between ourselves and others. It may be a physical, informational or emotional boundary between our public and personal life. Japanese people prefer to keep their personal and private life separate, so it is quite common for co-workers to know little about their colleagues' personal lives. Some prefer not to reveal their marital status or whether they are dating. Japanese stores like Maruzen book stores cater to this need for personal boundaries by asking customers whether or not they want a Maruzen book cover so that no one knows what book they are reading while on the train.

Maintaining our personal boundaries happens all over the world, in our cultures, our personal and professional lives. In teaching, counseling and coaching, we are taught to maintain a professional distance and to never reveal anything personal or to show any emotion. But in the end, we determine who we let into our personal worlds and how much of it they are allowed to see.

GENKAN: MOVE BETWEEN WORLDS

Moving between our private and public lives and spaces happens every day. It happens on our commutes to work, our journeys from point A to point B. The transition between these worlds can be subtle, gradual, and sometimes symbolic. *The Genkan*, the space in an entrance hall of a home or apartment, is one of these spaces. It is a holding area, a link between our outside world, our *omote*, and our inner, private world, our *ura*. In this space, we are greeted by our host, and take off our shoes once we are invited in. In her presentation *Designing Mindfulness: Spatial Concepts in Traditional Japanese Architecture*, Dr. Yoko Kawai, architect, space and wellness designer, and professor at Yale University, says that when guests arrive at the *genkan*, the guest is at ground level, while the host stands on the house floor, which is a foot higher. This gives the impression that the space is sacred for the host and we must be given verbal or nonverbal permission before we can step up onto that space before entering the home.

FIFTEEN PAUSES | TOM FRENGOS

JAPANESE GENKAN *OR HOLDING AREA*

Japanese folk tales suggest that this elevated space was used in old times to protect the owner from unwanted guests as it was easier to defend oneself if one was on the high ground. There are also suggestions that this elevated floor was created to signify status.

The *genkan* is a portal into another person's private world. Dr. Yoko Kawai, stated in her presentation that when we are at the *genkan* space, we have a limited view of the person's house as most of it is still hidden. Moving from the *genkan* space and going deeper into another person's place is a slow gradual process, as different aspects of the person's home are slowly revealed to us.

SPACE CAN BE NONNEGOTIABLE

Like the *genkan*, the sumo ring, or *dohyō*, is a sacred space for sumo wrestlers or anyone involved in the sport. It is considered the psychological, spiritual space where gods and demons do battle. Sumo has such high reverence for this space. There are strict rules for it, like how one enters it, when it can be entered and who is allowed to set foot on it. In 2018, in Kyoto, a politician was delivering a speech to an audience before a sumo exhibition match. While delivering his speech in the sumo ring, he collapsed suddenly. Men and women, including female nurses from the audience, rushed to the sumo ring to perform CPR. In the midst of this chaos, the referee asked all women to leave the sumo ring, despite the fact they were offering to help. In response to this incident, people on social media condemned the discrimination of women while others passionately protected sumo traditions. In the sumo ring, women are forbidden, by sumo tradition, from entering that 'sacred space' – no matter what.

Yet views about the *dohyō* space are changing. These days sumo tournaments for women are being held in Japan. The Netflix movie *Little Miss Sumo*, a 2018 documentary film directed and written by Matt Kay, shows how 20-year-old Hiyori Kon is leading this change. In Chapter 3, we'll look at how space, time and life are always changing even when we think nothing is happening.

TORI GATES: THRESHOLD SPACES

Japanese Shintō religion views space as sacred and essential to our lives. Some of the spaces act as thresholds. A *tori* (toh-ree) gate is one of those threshold spaces that brings you into a sacred space. When you walk towards a Shintō shrine, you will pass through a number of *tori* gates on the way to the shrine. The more *tori* gates you cross, the more sacred that space becomes. When entering a *tori* gate, it is customary to bow before entering that space.

TORI *GATE*

SHIMENAWA AND *YORISHIRO*: INVITING THE SPIRITS

In Shintō religion, there are other symbols that suggest a place is sacred. When you walk into a shrine, you will notice a special plaited rope hanging on a *tori* gate, a tree or a shrine. This is called a *shimenawa*.

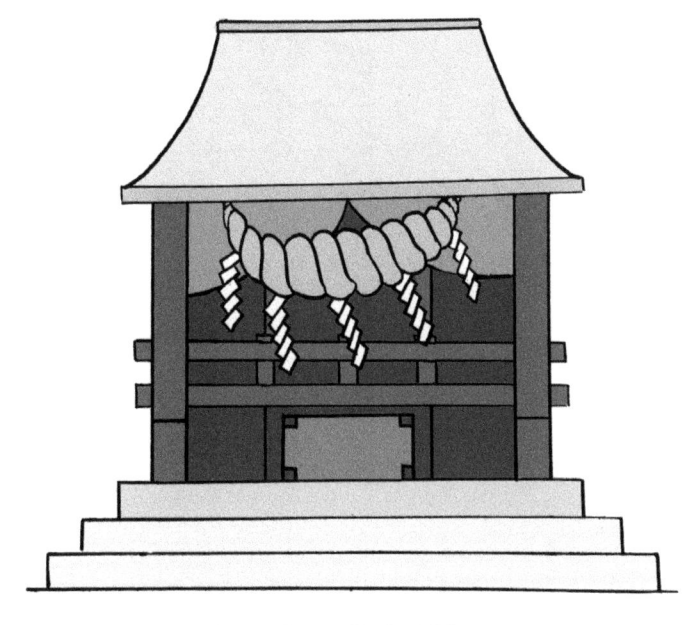

SHIMENAWA *ON SHRINE*

When it is tied around or across a shrine, a gate, a tree it becomes a *yorishiro*. This is a physical space that a spirit needs to enter and occupy for religious ceremonies or events. A *yorishiro* doesn't always become occupied by a spirit. It is up to the *kami* or spirit to enter it. You can also see a variation of a *shimenawa* in a sumo ring, a reminder that the space is sacred.

SHIMENAWA *ON TREE NEAR A SHRINE*

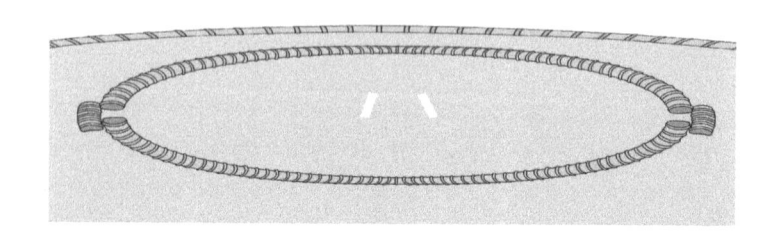

SHIMENAWA *ON SUMO RING OR* DOHYŌ

CHAPTER 2: SPACE IS SACRED AND MEANINGFUL

In sumo, the highest-ranking sumo wrestler, the *Yokozuna* is considered to be a living *yorishiro* who wears a variation of a *shimenawa* to attract a spirit to reside within them.

SUMO WRESTLER WEARING VARIATION OF SHIMENAWA

SHINTAI: WHERE SPIRITS LIVE

When a *kami* or spirit enters the empty space of a *yorishiro* and occupies it, it becomes a *shintai*, a place where spirits dwell. A *Yokozuna* can also become a *shintai*. Yet this dwelling is never permanent. Spirits can come and go at any time. A *shintai* is often located at or near a Shintō shrine. Mount Fuji is also considered a *shintai*. It is one of the reasons why many Japanese people consider the trek to Mount Fuji to be a spiritual pilgrimage.

WE BECOME MINDFUL IN JAPANESE SPACE

Japanese architects also believe in the sanctity of spaces. Space is a catalyst that creates a dialogue between human beings and all living things. It invites us to pause in silence to reflect, to bring people together to collaborate, to discover something meaningful. It is a sense of place that awakens our feelings of belonging. It is so powerful and so alluring that it draws us in, encourages us to stay in the present. In her presentation *Designing Mindfulness*, Dr. Yoko Kawai says that traditional Japanese architecture facilitates mindfulness. It encourages us to slow down and enjoy the gift of life.

A traditional Japanese teahouse also evokes mindfulness. As you walk towards the teahouse, you may need to walk through a *roji* pathway, a meandering pathway of randomly spaced stones that forces you to be mindful of your steps. As you focus on the stones and the surroundings around you, you break your ties with the outside world and enter a new one.

CHAPTER 2: SPACE IS SACRED AND MEANINGFUL

ROJI *PATHWAY TO TEAHOUSE*

The Comico Art Museum in the onsen town Yufuin, designed by architect Kengo Kuma, is another example of that mindfulness. As you enter the museum on the first floor, you will notice that exhibit I and II are separated by two glass walls, and between those walls is a gap filled with a rivulet of water. You can see what is on the other side, but you can't directly walk across to exhibit II. That entrance is on the other side of the building. To get there, you must go outside and walk along an approach flanked by bushes, bamboo, trees and rocks from the local area. Walking along this meditative approach prepares you for the second exhibit on the other side.

But your journey is far from over. There is a staircase that takes you to the final exhibit on the second floor that has a courtyard where you can stand and appreciate a view of Mount Yufu and see Yufuin's newest landmark – Yoshimoto Nara's *Your Dog* exhibit. As you look at it, this dog looks as if it is peacefully watching over that mountain.

Waking this pathway and climbing these steps encourages us to pay attention to what is in front of us right now, to observe nature surrounding this building, to appreciate the harmony between nature and architecture. Comico Art Museum reminds us to enjoy our journey from one exhibit to another. It graciously and gently places us in life's slow lane.

EMPTY SPACES MAKE US NOSTALGIC

In mid-February 2020, the Japanese salary person went into the remote working world. Many of them were working in a small space in their living room dedicated to work, but it wasn't their office. This space they were sitting in, tucked away in a small corner of their home was quiet, temporary and empty. There was no one next to them to share an idea, to provide support, or to tell a joke. The constant hum of noise, the chatter of co-workers and the endless clicks of the nearby computer keyboards, the morning exercise rituals, the announcements and celebrations of achieving milestones, the daily chit chats with their colleagues, the meetings, the lunches together and even the bad times – all of that was gone. The shared space they used to work in gave them a purpose, an identity, a sense of belonging, a reason to get up in the morning.

The year 2020 made us more aware of why our work space is important to us. While many of us couldn't return to the office right away, we could still imagine and reflect on that space we left behind. We remember the corner of our desk where we have our coffee, the partition behind our computer that shows a picture of our loved ones or a medal or award we received for our dedication and hard work.

This nostalgic thinking allows us to travel back in time, to recall what we left behind. Nostalgia brings that space and time to life once again. Pausing in that empty space or pausing to remember it from afar allows the memories of that space and place to come back to us. We learn to value that space, to fondly remember the days and acts that define us. We recall the face-to-face conversations, the work, the rituals we did together. Nostalgia also brings us ideas for the future, like how we can take some of the past, the work, the rituals, those valued conversations, and transport it into these new spaces.

A space without meaning can be unsettling. This is why many people around the world were struggling with working remotely early in 2020. So how do we transform a space that is barren, meaningless into one that means something, a place where we belong, somewhere that reinforces our identity as a worker? In Chapter 12, I will talk about the rituals we can use for creating meaning in these spaces.

IN-BETWEEN SPACES MATTER

Human beings dislike those spaces between where we were and where want to be. We find them on a long-haul flight, in meetings we don't want to be in, on the way work and on a crowded train.

When we are unable to leave these spaces, we distract ourselves to make this time bearable. We look down at our phones or chat to friends while waiting at the lights, or we post something to our Instagram followers while our train crosses a bridge over a once-in-a-life-time sight. We daydream, forget about the people in front of us. We think about where we would rather be. Yet it turns out that these in-between spaces we think are boring, stressful, empty, meaningless, actually do matter!

These spaces are where we make friends, take up a new hobby, learn a language, approach a Shinto shrine, create something, transition between lives, fall in love, discover a new calling, enjoy life. They are also where feel stagnant, where we argue, struggle, suffer, and yet in these imperfect spaces and moments we grow the most.

A research journal article titled: *'My drive is my sacred time': commuting as routine liminality* revealed that while many of us find commutes stressful and inconvenient, there are many of us who find value in them. These in-between spaces give us the time to read a book, think about our lives, learn a language. They are more important than we thought.

Too often we take these spaces for granted, until we are out of them. The *Great Pause* I hope, reminded us that the spaces we occupy in the present are just as important as the ones we just came from and are rushing towards. When we stop and think about them more, we discover these spaces are the fertile grounds that accept the seeds of our present and allow them to blossom into our memories.

PART II:
Our mental, emotional and social pauses

CHAPTER 3:
Change is an eternal dance

Moment after moment everything comes out from nothingness. This is the true joy of life.
– Shunryu Suzuki

The truths of life slowly reveal themselves in a pause. I found them every time I looked out at the world from my balcony in 2020.

In late March, 2020, the Japanese cherry blossom season had finally arrived in Fukuoka. Pinkish white coloured blossoms were now blooming around me, their presence filled me with a youthful energy, an energizing hope, a gratitude to witness one of nature's greatest shows from my balcony.

A week later, the spring winds blew these blossoms off the tree, breaking them apart one by one into lonely single pink petals. They swirled upward, downward, and into the clear blue sky, but soon these petals relented. They fluttered back down to earth slowly, gently landing on their final resting place – a pinkish white carpet of other fallen, departed cherry blossom petals.

Green serrated leaves replaced these fallen blossoms; they generously formed a thick canopy that protected us from the relentless hot summer months of July and August. Birds and cicadas now arrived at their seasonal home – a small home – yet both life forms coexisted, even during the hottest days of the summer when this tree became a rock concert venue. On those hot days, cicadas screamed out their deafening love songs as they frantically searched for a mate before they died a week later.

Towards the end of August, these cicadas died one by one; their lifeless husks fell to the ground, their remains scattered around the base of the tree – a daily reminder of the life that once thrived in this tree, but will never again this year. Birds began singing their melancholy songs. Perhaps they and the tree were mourning the departure of their cicada friends. Even I was mourning their absence.

But that mourning was brief. In early September, a great typhoon battered its way up from the Okinawan islands, reaching Fukuoka the next day, bringing with it pelting rain and ferocious 140 km/hr winds that rattled this tree so violently I thought it would be blown away. Yet this proud, brave cherry blossom tree remained strong, unbroken by this great typhoon.

In mid-September, the rains stopped and the cicadas were gone. The tree became soothingly quiet once again – yet something was about to happen. With less warmth, less sunlight, and now shorter days and much colder evening air arriving, this tree changed again. Green leaves gradually transformed into brilliant autumn red fiery leaves. Nature's final act of the year was about to begin – and I had a front row seat.

In November, birds abandoned this tree in favour of a warmer one further south. Leaves, once fiery red but now fading in colour, fell to wither and die. These fallen leaves scattered all over the ground, their rustling noise sounded like another sombre ballad, this time weeping for an empty tree that would be alone for the long, cold winter. A brief icy wind immediately came and shook the empty, lonely tree – a reminder of the cold taste of winter that would soon arrive.

In January, a rare snowfall came. Snowflakes swirled in between the branches, falling and resting on the tree's base. They clung valiantly to the tree until they melted away when the sun emerged from behind the cold thick winter clouds.

The tree was empty again but something was happening. Inside, nutrients were spreading throughout the tree. They were nourishing the tree, producing buds that slowly appeared one by one on this tree. Soon they would open for the next cherry blossom season.

Something is always happening with this cherry blossom tree. It's always changing, blooming, emptying, refilling with life. I never grow tired of this story, no matter how many times I see it.

MA SPACE IS A MOVING BOUNDARY

Japanese Zen Buddhism believes life is in constant motion, always changing, and that nothing is permanent. The space between the walls of a building, the distance between us in the physical and online space, the atmosphere in that space – all of this is changing. As we sit and wait, we think nothing is happening, yet something IS happening. Seasons change, the sun rises and sets. Shadows fill the space of an open room, move across it, then fade away. Flowers bloom, die, people and animals leave and enter an empty space. Sun and moonlight shine between these gates. Ma is waiting for change to happen naturally, and not trying to force it before its time.

SOMETHING IS ALWAYS HAPPENING IN OUR LIVES

For a while, I had nothing to write for this section. Then as I was making myself a coffee, I thought of my hometown return to Canada in 2018. It was a cold February day with the temperature being -10°C. Snow was swirling around us. As I was walking away from my car, I ran into one of my friends who was leaving a restaurant.

My friend is ambitious. He has been quite successful in his roles as a salesperson and sales manager in the tech industry. Whenever I meet him, he is always buzzing with infectious energy. He is always excited about his work, wanting to talk about it, like how he's starting a new business. He is always doing something.

As I was stomping my feet in one spot trying to keep myself warm, he asked me what I was doing in Japan. Eager to move into the warm restaurant ahead, I gave him the executive summary, telling him that I was travelling around the country and learning the language.

He looked surprised and offered his summary of my year: "So you are doing nothing there."

I smiled and replied, "And loving it."

I said my goodbye, promised to catch up with him the following week, and then hurried into the restaurant for a hot chocolate.

For me, 2018, my year of nothing, was my most valuable time in Japan. The prospect of finding work in April was a bit low. I had returned from a 6-week stay in Canada. I was excited by the thought of what life would offer me in 2018. I was in no hurry to go back to the work I'd left behind in Australia, the year before. I finished writing a chapter for an academic book. I wanted a break from writing. I wanted something else, but nothing came to mind.

In February 2018, while still in Canada, I searched the internet, looking for something to do once I returned to Japan. I came across two conferences about Japanese culture that would be worth presenting at. I now had a new project, something I was passionate about. I felt re-inspired.

Later that year, I worked in a mountain hut on Mt Fuji for 8 weeks, doing hard manual labour carrying supplies of 30 kilograms each at nearly 2800 meters above sea level and waiting endlessly on climbers flowing in and out of the mountain hut. All of this was a test of my humility. For a year that started off as a nothing year, it sure filled up with a lot of interesting projects and adventures.

In 2020, I thought about how many people had lost their jobs or taken time off, how many people were feeling like they weren't doing anything because they weren't working, how many people felt they weren't contributing to society.

When transitioning between jobs, careers, lives, we have this fear that if we aren't doing something like attending a job interview, making money, being seen or heard in society, in groups, on social media, we are doing nothing. Doing nothing, we think, invalidates us. We fear that DOING nothing means we ARE nothing!

In this time of personal transitions, many of my friends and family were finding something. We were creating, learning, forming relationships, exploring new lifestyles. Many people were doing pro bono work, teaching people English, counseling people. During this time, we stopped and reflected on where we were headed, what we wanted to do. This was a reset, a time to start from nothing.

Many people were starting new careers, opening up new businesses, even coffee shops. A new career can come out of the blue, brought on by a passing thought, a comment made by a friend that we should open up a coffee shop, or write a book. In the business world, a good idea can sometimes emerge out of nowhere, without any other precedent. It can be adopted, but when some other idea comes along, that brilliant idea becomes obsolete. New meaning can emerge in this space of Ma, where we think there is no meaning in this space of transition, no joy in our work or our lives.

In Leonard Koren's book *Wabi-Sabi for Artists, Designers, Poets and Philosophers*, he writes: "Things are either devolving toward, or evolving from, nothingness."

The life of a cherry blossom tree embodies this move from nothingness into something. Cherry blossoms emerge out of nothing to become cherry blossom flowers, then dissolve back into nothingness. The trees then renew with new flowers and these flowers dissolve into nothingness again. Something is always happening in our lives and in the world, even if people are telling us otherwise.

JAPANESE NOH THEATER: RETURN TO EMPTINESS

Japanese Noh theatre is one of the oldest forms of theatre in the world, dating back to the 14th century. It is UNESCO listed as an Intangible Cultural Heritage. Noh theatre is well known for its sense of Ma. Before the play starts, spectators see an empty stage with no props. This emptiness creates an excitement, tension as we wait for something to happen. Emptiness makes us taut and expectant.

EMPTY NOH THEATRE STAGE

CHAPTER 3: CHANGE IS AN ETERNAL DANCE

When the play starts, one by one, musicians enter the stage though a backdoor. The actors enter slowly via a main bridge called a Hashigakari. This bridge symbolizes the transition from the world of the dead to the world of the living, the stage. When the performance is over, the stage is cleared again slowly, reverting to its original form of emptiness.

ENTERING THE NOH THEATRE STAGE

CROSSING THE HASHIGAKARI

BEAUTY IS BORN OUT OF SILENCE

Zen Buddhism believes silence is essential to the daily rhythm of life. Silence heightens our attention and awakens our senses. It makes us more present to what we are doing in the moment, respect the space we are in. I went to Tochoji temple in Fukuoka in 2018 for the cherry blossom season. I remember watching, through the branches of the cherry blossom tree, a woman gazing at the cherry blossom tree. Her transfixed eyes were following the fluttering petals as they were falling to the ground. I remember her subtle sigh that followed as they fell below her line of sight. I remember the silence and feeling that echoed after that.

CHAPTER 3: CHANGE IS AN ETERNAL DANCE

WATCHING THE CHERRY BLOSSOMS FALL

Silence moves us. It inspires us to transcend words, to go beyond the boundaries of our conscious minds, our tendency to describe and label what we see. If we start describing or analyzing the experience of the falling blossom trees, we miss out on the true experience, its ability to move us emotionally. Silence uses our full senses, our sense of taste, sound, smell, touch and sight. In this silence, we see the world as it is. We marvel in its beauty, and pay more attention to the life-changing messages the world sends to us in silence.

EXHILARATING, FRIGHTENING SILENCE

Silence at first seems uncomfortable. It awakens our insecurities, our attachment to our language, our need to say something, our need to prove we know what we are talking about, our need to do something. Silence evokes a feeling of nonbeing and vulnerability.

In 2018, after finishing my summer work on Mount Fuji, I took a bus from Kawaguchiko Station to Aokigahara Jukai, meaning the sea of trees. Aokigahara is a massive forest on north-western flank of Mount Fuji in Yamanashi prefecture. It is 30 square kilometers and rests on solidified lava that was created from Mount Fuji's last major eruption in 864 CE.

Aokigahara is infamously known as the suicide forest. Movies, literature and social media circles have created a bad meaning for this place, how walking in a silent forest alone is scary, a place that some people never return from. I remember getting concerned looks when I was asking for directions on how to get there and which bus to take.

One local woman asked me, " Why do you want to go there?"

I reassured her with a look of optimism, "It's okay. I am coming back."

As I jumped into the bus, I looked back. She still looked concerned.

Aokigahara is very quiet. I couldn't hear any birds, any insects. This is because the porous lava rock absorbs sound. Walking through this quiet forest, I felt exposed to something but I couldn't put into words what that was. It was me and the forest. Nothing else existed. This feeling was addictive, so much I was keen to return to this sanctuary.

In January 2020, I returned to Aokigahara with my friends, one of them being a local tour guide to this place. It was -4°C. Snow sparsely covered the tracks we walked on. We trekked through a different part of the forest and then climbed down into an ice cave. Inside it was quite dark. Our head lamps could only light up the five meters in front of us. Walking slowly and carefully up and down the slippery steps, we arrived at the bottom after nearly 30 minutes of coldness. Our guide asked us to turn off our headlamps, stand in this dark, and say nothing.

As we stood in this darkness in silence, I felt the cold air more. I heard the soothing sounds of ice melting and dropping to the ground. Then it stopped. There was no sound at all. Nothing. I couldn't hear myself breathing. I couldn't see my breath. I wanted to turn on my light, to say something. That feeling gave way to calmness. I am unable to recall another experience so confusing, so frightening and yet exhilarating – all in one moment.

SILENCE RELEASES US

Liberating silence is all around us. It is in a Zen retreat, an ice cave. It is in Japanese arts, even in a play or music. Musicians who use *shakuhachi* or Japanese flutes often add silence into their piece. This pause in music creates tension, excitement. It makes us engage with the performer more. We wonder when they are going to restart. In Western countries we use a moment of silence in a sporting event, before the competition begins, to remember someone who has passed away. Silence allows us to privately connect with our own emotions and remember these people in our own way.

Silence is important to our health and well-being. Researchers from the University of Pavia in Italy and Oxford University in the United Kingdom studied cardiovascular and respiratory responses in both musicians and nonmusicians to fast music. They randomly inserted a two-minute pause in a musical piece. Results report that music with a faster tempo and simple rhythms significantly increased breathing rate and heart rate. On the other hand, the pause reduced heart rate and blood pressure. It relaxed breathing, even below baseline, particularly for those with music training. While fast music can arouse people, a pause releases them from that arousal.

ANSWERS SHINE IN A PAUSE

We use silence to communicate. We even use it to highlight an important point. Famous Western leaders like Elon Musk would often pause and stew in silence for a dozen seconds before answering a serious question in interviews. In presentations, Steve Jobs would pause before giving answers to challenging questions from the audience.

Long pauses before answers are given can feel awkward. Our minds fill this space and time with our own thoughts. We incorrectly assume that the presenter doesn't know the answer or they are annoyed with us. Silence is uncomfortable. We must break that silence at all costs. Or so we think.

Silence can also mean we are thinking deeply about a response, even respecting the question. It is the beacon that shines between the question and the answer, makes the answer more important, invites the audience to think deeply, tune in more to the presenter, and wait for that answer. Silence makes us appreciate the answer more, the work and the journey the speaker has gone through to deliver the answer to us. Without it, answers may seem trivial, hurried and unimportant. An answer needs silence to shine!

SILENCE REFINES OUR WORDS

Japanese film director Ryûsuke Hamaguchi director of the movie *Drive My Car*, which won an Academy Award for Best International Feature Film in 2022, uses silence in his movies. In his video interview for Film at Lincoln Center, he explained (through his translator):

> Silence is an attitude, an ability to patiently wait even when we may think nothing is happening. But something is happening. There is a beautiful, internal struggle to search for the right words, a time to refine them, a chance to carefully select the right ones.

According to Ryûsuke Hamaguchi, we are finding our clear voice in silence, creating a "rich form of communication" we didn't have before the pause started. Chapter 12 will further explain how staying in that silence is transformative.

SILENCE AND NOISE ARE ETERNALLY JOINED

A silence of Ma is good for our health but so are verbal communication and noise. We need nonsilence to communicate with each other, to entertain, to express ourselves, to feel belonging when silence doesn't do the trick. Like in music and performances, we all need that balance between silence and nonsilence. It is those moments of noise we crave for silence to refresh and heal. It is those moments of silence we crave for a return to noise and conversation.

On a silent September 2020 morning, I was concentrating deeply on my book, and enjoying the blissful silence. That silence was suddenly interrupted by the sounds of an airplane taking off from the nearby Hakata airport, followed by the grinding revving sounds of a delivery truck idling as the delivery person dropped off supplies to the nursing home in front of my apartment. I am unsure as to when exactly it happened, but my frustration with this noise changed into a delight. I smiled as I heard the laughs of the kids nearby and the roaring of the delivery truck picking speed as it left the parking lot. All of this, for one moment, reminded me life still goes on.

MA IS AN ETERNAL DANCE

The space between the walls of a building, the physical and online distance between us – all of this is changing. It may not have meaning at first, but it will have meaning when we pause, wait for change to happen, reflect on what we do in that space and who we are. The next time you look at an empty space where you feel nothing, hear nothing and see nothing, you may see something more profound, a reminder of what the world really is about. Ma is pausing in the space and gratefully watching the eternal union of something with nothing, emptiness with fullness, silence with sound. It is an unlikely, graceful dance between improbable partners that makes the world whole.

CHAPTER 4:

Mikansei – incompleteness is beautiful

One hundred attempts, One thousand improvements.
  – **Senzaburo Miura**
  Hiroshima's Ginjo sake pioneer

The best things in life shouldn't be rushed – like Hiroshima sake. When I drank my first cup of Hiroshima sake, I discovered that perfection has no deadline – it never should.

In Hiroshima, in the late 19th century, Senzaburo Miura, who was running a family grocery business, decided to start a sake business. Wanting to learn from the best, he set up new facilities in the Kobe suburb of Nada – the center of the sake universe. Senzaburo hired the best brew masters, learned the Nada brewing techniques. He then took that knowledge back to Hiroshima. Yet, when he used these techniques, he was getting bad sake for four years. This led to him closing down the sake part of the business.

He didn't give up. He investigated why he was getting bad sake; he tried to improve the process. He then went

CHAPTER 4: *MIKANSEI* - INCOMPLETENESS IS BEAUTIFUL

to Fushimi in Kyoto, another great sake region, where he learned there was one thing he couldn't change – the water. Hiroshima and Fushimi, like most of Japan, has soft water, which was unsuitable for the sake brewing methods he was using.

Senzaburo's brewing process was right for Nada but not for Hiroshima and Fushimi. Nada breweries used hard water from Mount Rokko in Kobe, one of the few places in Japan with hard water. Hard water is mineral rich and ideal for sake brewing, but it rushes the process; it doesn't easily bring out the refreshing tastes and aroma we find in the more refined sakes.

After years of failing, testing and revising, Senzaburo Miura pioneered a new scientific method for soft-water brewing. He slowly brewed the sake, at lower temperatures. This brought out the gentle, delicate flavours that are now characteristic of Hiroshima's Ginjo sake. It took 20 years for him to perfect this method, and when he did, it was made available to other Hiroshima breweries and other breweries around Japan. Anyone who loves Ginjo sake has Senzaburo Miura to thank.

Before he passed away in 1908, Senzaburo left behind his secret to his successful brewing technique. It was *hyakushi senkai*, which means "a hundred attempts, a thousand improvements." One interesting observation here. The fourth Japanese *kanji* character (bottom left), pronounced kai, is the same first character used for the word *Kaizen* – the Toyota word for continuous improvement.

HYAKUSHI SENKAI: *A HUNDRED ATTEMPTS, A THOUSAND IMPROVEMENTS*

MA IS THE INCOMPLETE JOURNEY

As you continue this journey towards mastering Ma, your views of it may be changing. Ma is more than just a space between people, a pause or a silence. It is the beginning and end of a project, a commute to work, a climb up a mountain, a sporting competition, a journey in self-discovery. It is living in that moment, enjoying the journey but that's difficult to maintain when that goal waiting for us at the end is so appealing and alluring that we stop concentrating on the present task. We daydream about the achievement; we rush to finish things quickly rather than giving ourselves enough time to get it right. We feel pressured to meet a deadline, to win approval from others and validate our worth.

In a world that demands closure and results, Ma offers us an alternative lifestyle. There is no need to rush and finish things right away just because people are telling us this or we believe it to be so. We can enjoy the process of reaching our goals rather than getting to the end. Ma is living the life of a painter in search of painting their best work, yet in no hurry to finish it. We discover that there is still paint and magic left in our paint brush to complete our masterpiece.

ELEVATOR PITCHES NEED TIME

In May 2021, someone said to me if I didn't have an elevator pitch for this book, no one would buy it. I had been researching Ma for 3 years, and writing about it for a year, but my elevator pitch was non-existent. I felt pressure to have this pitch right away, yet I still needed time to form one that I felt comfortable with.

I remember mentioning my book to another coach at an online seminar in a small Zoom breakout room in June 2021. Ma intrigued her. It was perfect for her work. Yet she didn't want to hear too many details. She only wanted a 3 x 5 cheat sheet, and a 15 second summary that she could immediately use with her clients. Ma was relevant to my work as a coach as well, but I was reluctant to say much because I was still trying to figure out it myself, even though I was writing a book on it. I still needed more time to learn about Ma, perfect it before I could get on the elevator and deliver that pitch.

MIKANSEI: INCOMPLETENESS IS BEAUTIFUL

In 2017, I discovered the word *mikansei* from Boyé Lafayette De Mente's book, *The Japanese have a word for it*. Mikansei (mee-kan-seh-ee), according to Boyé Lafayette De Mente, means the power of incompleteness. We experience *mikansei* in daily life in an incomplete explanation or an incomplete piece of art. Japanese carpenters will leave some wood furnishings incomplete, they won't add the finishing touches of lacquer. Artists and architects will stop short of finishing a piece of art, a room, a drawing or a Japanese character.

In Zen philosophy, incompleteness encourages us to fill in the gaps. It personalizes the space when we add our own ideas to the puzzle that life offers us. *Mikansei* is often used in Japanese brainstorming meetings where an incomplete idea, or a rough draft is presented and then ideas are added and enhancements are made by other people. If a manager gives an incomplete project for people to complete, the people become collectively energized to complete it.

Mikansei is present in nature. On a full moon night, the moon may be partially hiding behind a building, a forest or a cloud. We then wonder what that complete view of the moon looks like. We long for that moon to come out from the shadows, to rise above the mountain ridge, or break free from the thick storm clouds. Yet we still, paradoxically, want to stay in this space, and hold onto that feeling of longing.

CHAPTER 4: *MIKANSEI* - INCOMPLETENESS IS BEAUTIFUL

CHALLENGE YOUR NEED TO BE FIRST

Being first drives us. We feel compelled to say something, to write something before someone else does. If we remain silent, hold off writing something then we lose our chance to be the first to the market, to be the expert, to grow our business before our competition does. Our world values people and organizations that are the first to give us up-to-date knowledge. It admires people who always seem to have all the answers when others are still scratching their heads. For writers who are still searching for answers, we may feel like amateurs, someone who hasn't yet published, someone who had potential but never achieved.

It is human nature to want immediate answers, elevator pitches and accomplishments. Yet we also have that capacity to stop and ask ourselves, do we publish right away for the sake of being first? Should we wait a bit longer instead and get it right? *Mikansei* inspires us to stop and enjoy that incompleteness, to enjoy learning something new, to keep digging for more research, to happily slow down and analyze our facts, to double check those facts before publishing them.

PROJECT MANAGERS AND MA: FRIENDS OR FOES?

As I was writing this chapter, I thought about project managers. Do they like Ma? Their job is about managing a project but, mostly, it's about getting it done. If they don't get it done, and on time, then they wouldn't be a project manager for very long. My gut instinct, past experiences and conversations with clients suggested that project managers and Ma were bitter foes.

When I spoke to my client about the concept of Ma, she immediately recalled a consulting project she did in Sydney, Australia, almost 10 years ago. On the first day, her project manager (let's call him Bob) checked her progress every hour. Later, when she went out for lunch with one of the other contractors, she was given the dirty little secrets about the project so far. According to her colleague, who had been with the project since its beginning, the previous contractors were a disappointment. They were hired quickly without a proper vetting of their experience and qualifications. Milestones and deadlines were missed. Poor work was done. They were fired. Past contractors and the impact created bad Ma for this project. The project manager, Bob, had become more controlling over many things. She chuckled as she described how her team couldn't openly brainstorm ideas with other colleagues sitting right next to each other. Bob's reasoning – there was no time for chit chat.

Every hour, Bob would check his milestone spreadsheet, then turning to face his team he would ask them how they were progressing with their milestones and why they were behind schedule, even if it were for only an hour. My client continued, telling me how, during her lunch break, Bob's anxious eyes would follow her to the door. It was even worse when she went out with another colleague at the same time. She even remembered getting death stares from Bob when she and her colleague both returned after a 10-minute coffee break. She laughs about it now every time she tells this story.

According to my client, a project manager that is distrustful of others and constantly looking for closure doesn't like Ma. It is a threat to their role, their identity. The uncertainty of whether people will meet their timelines, the incompleteness, the state of unknowing – all of this can give them fits. She cautions anyone working with such project managers. They will pressure you to commit to a timeline that you feel uncomfortable with. If you don't achieve that timeline, they will remind you that you were the one who set that deadline. You may find yourself frantically working faster to get to that milestone to please the project manager, to win their trust and approval.

She happily told me that after 5 weeks on the project, she had enough of this environment and left. Luckily for her, she immediately found a new role and happily worked with a project manager who had a friendlier, more Zen-like outlook towards Ma.

DO YOU HAVE A HIGH NEED FOR CLOSURE?

When we are waiting, life can become stressful even scary because we don't know what the future holds. Waiting awakens our need for closure, our need to know, our need to finish something, our need to have finality.

Our need for closure, made famous by social psychologist Arie Kruglanski in the 1990s, is the need for a definite answer to a question or a problem, as opposed to uncertainty, confusion, or ambiguity. A high need for closure drives us to make quick decisions, sometimes frantically search for knowledge to reduce that confusion and ambiguity, to look for the most available answer, even if it is not the right one for us. Our need for closure can make us settle for the first bit of news that comes our way, treat it as true and complete, even though it may be false and incomplete.

Our need for closure can skew the facts or make us rush into making premature judgements, perhaps even when moving to a new country. A 2004 study by Tomoko Masumoto on American interns working in Japanese companies for 6 months found that interns became frustrated with their Japanese managers' lack of feedback on their performance and made quick assumptions about this. The interns concluded that their managers weren't being honest, not doing their job, and possibly that all Japanese supervisors were the same.

I like to think culture is more complicated than that. I believe that it is possible that many new arrivals to Japan can also make quick assumptions about their newly adopted culture, sometimes negative ones, especially when things aren't going well. A new country creates uncertainty. We try to reduce that uncertainty by forming conclusions about how other cultures and other people think and act, on the basis of a few people. When we prefer closure, we think that a few experiences with a few people are enough to go on.

If these interns working in Japan had suspended their initial judgments about Japanese managers, they may have found that a lack of feedback may not always have a bad intent behind it. Lack of feedback doesn't mean people were doing a poor job. In Japan, there is no need to tell people they are doing a good job, as it should be obvious.

Mikansei puts the brakes on our search for self-validation, our need to know everything. In a way, it encourages us to accept uncertainty and the things that are out of our control.

EMBRACE UNCERTAINTY

Living with uncertainty can be hard when it involves someone we love. In their US study on managing uncertainty in a mid-western US hospital waiting room, researchers Anne Stone and John Lammers found that sitting in the waiting room while loved ones are in surgery is indeed an anxious uncertain time for family members. Their study revealed that family members managed this anxious time differently. Most waited patiently or found something to manage that anxiety. They distracted themselves by speaking to or texting family or friends on the progress of surgery, watching the tv in the waiting room or reading something. But some were less patient. They walked back and forth from the waiting room to the front desk to check with the doctors and nurses nearly every 15 minutes to see that everything was okay or ask staff why it was taking so long.

While it wasn't reported in this article, I can speak from my own experience that if the anxiety is high, our anxious minds transport us to two possible futures, thinking it may relieve that anxiety. In the positive future, we imagine the surgery is successful, our loved one is recovering, and we will be with them again. In the worst-case future scenario, we imagine losing our loved one and feel regret for not saying a proper goodbye.

So how else can we manage this uncertainty, prevent ourselves from thinking the worst? In this same study, researchers found that hospital staff helped reduce that uncertainty by giving families as much information as possible on the procedure, like how long it will take and who the surgeon will be. Hospital volunteers also employed distraction tactics, where they would talk to the families about non-medical topics such as local social events, anything to forget about the surgery, even for a few minutes. Hospital volunteers also provided reassurance, especially if a surgery was taking longer than expected. In that case, hospital volunteers reassured families in the waiting room that no news doesn't always mean bad news and later than expected doesn't mean something bad has happened. A final strategy was providing assistance like directing or escorting families to the postoperative floor where their loved one was recovering.

How else can we manage this waiting? As for me, I try reading a book, watching television, going for dinner – anything that can distract me and keep me in the present moment.

It's worth noting that no matter how much support and information we receive about a surgery there will always be uncertainty. In these moments of uncertainty, we are unable to control the outcome all the time, but we can control how we respond and wait – we can learn to have faith, accept an uncertain future that is out of our hands.

FOCUS ONE POINT AT A TIME

Staying in the moment, that time and space between a beginning and end, is fragile. No matter how much meditation and mindfulness we use to keep us in the moment, something in the future that is more attractive and more appealing can whisk our minds into the future if we aren't careful.

In the 1990 Wimbledon tennis championships, three time Wimbledon champion Boris Becker from Germany faced his friend and rival, Swedish player Stefan Edberg, for the third consecutive year. Edberg had won their first Wimbledon final in 1988 while Becker won in 1989. In this 1990 championship Becker fell behind 2 sets to love in a best of 5 set final. Becker fought back to level the match at 2 sets all. In the fifth set, Becker broke Edberg's serve to go up 3-1 in the final set, and it looked like he would complete the comeback.

In the next game Stefan Edberg immediately broke Boris Becker's serve, then won four of the last five games to win the final set 6-4 and steal the title away from Becker. In the Wimbledon video: *The Trilogy | When Edberg and Becker Headlined Wimbledon*, Boris Becker revealed that when he was up 3-1 in the final set, he thought the match was his. He began to imagine what it was going to feel like when he won.

So how do we learn to stay in the moment when all we want to do is to hold the trophy? In tennis, players are taught to focus on one point at a time. 2021 Wimbledon champion, Australian Ashleigh Barty, said her way of staying in the match is the enjoyment of the match rather than the conclusion. She loves the match, the struggle. She loves pushing herself. Perhaps if we can all learn to find enjoyment in the process, to enjoy the encouragement and applause from the crowd more than the end, we are more likely to stay in that moment.

In Japanese martial arts, martial artists focus on their moves and their opponent only and not the victory. Thinking of victory is a recipe for disaster. In the business world, we may focus so hard on getting a project done that we rush through it, forget things and make mistakes. Even as I was writing this book, I was feeling pulled to the finish line because I believed the book was needed right away. In sports, life and work, Mikansei changes the rules of the game. The uncertain moments over who wins or who loses are more defining and more exciting than the moment we lift that trophy above our heads.

READ MORE NOVELS

There are times when closure is unnecessary. Nonclosure can be a good thing. It keeps us thinking, gives us more time to be creative. Researchers at the University of Toronto conducted a study on how to reduce the need for cognitive closure. In their study, 100 participants were assigned to read either fictional short stories or nonfictional essays. The results showed that when reading short stories, participants reported a decrease in the need for cognitive closure. This was especially evident for habitual readers (of either fiction or nonfiction). Short stories sometimes have an incomplete ending. They leave you thinking there must more to the story, that it is not over. A story without an ending can be poetic.

INCOMPLETE SENTENCES ARE POETIC

Mikansei is everywhere in Japanese conversations. It is present when feelings aren't verbally expressed, when explanations are left vague or sentences are unfinished. Japanese people have learned to decode these unfinished sentences, these unspoken words and feelings.

In the movie *The Last Samurai*, Tom Cruise's character Nathan Algren meets with Samurai leader Katsumoto, played by Ken Watanabe, in a courtyard filled with cherry blossom trees. They talk about Algren's nightmares, the fragility of life, the concept of *Bushido*, which means the way of the warrior. As Katsumoto tells Algren that they will go to Tokyo to meet with the emperor, Katsumoto's assistant returns to the courtyard with Algren's book, which was taken from him when he was captured. Katsumoto returns it to him with the following words:

"When I took this from you, you were my enemy."

Katsumoto turns quickly and walks away, leaving Algren alone in silence, in the courtyard. Most people watching this know that he means that Algren is no longer his enemy, but there's no need to state it. An incomplete sentence gives us an ambiguous feeling. Yet, it heightens the bond, because we intuitively understand what the person means. In close relationships, there's no need to finish another person's sentence to show we understand. *Mikansei* is the poetic empathy that comes out of these ambiguous, unfinished conversations.

DRAW A ZEN CIRCLE

An incomplete Zen circle called an *ensō*. That's what helped me complete this chapter.

JAPANESE ENSŌ

CHAPTER 4: *MIKANSEI* - INCOMPLETENESS IS BEAUTIFUL

An *ensō* never lies. Completed decisively in one single stroke, it says a lot about who we are at that moment. It is difficult to hide anything in an *ensō*. Whatever we are trying to hide, it is soon revealed in the way we paint that circle, how we hold our brush, how smooth, how full and how fast we complete this stroke. Doing an *ensō* quickly suggests we are in a rush to get things done, while doing it slowly and calmly suggests an enjoyment of the process rather than the outcome. A complete circle suggests we have reached enlightenment – that perfection or sense of mastery. An incomplete circle like the one I have drawn means our journey isn't yet done and we still have more to learn. We complete the circle when we are ready.

A DESTINATION WE MAY NEVER REACH

When something is incomplete, we continue to think about it. We want to finish it and yet perfect it. We dream about the accomplishment we will feel and the rewards and accolades we will receive when we are done. Closure gives us finality, but does focusing too much on the cherished finish line help us all the time?

Ma transcends our need for completeness. Incompleteness is a necessary seed for completeness, which isn't permanent at all. No matter how often we try to close things, there will always be something to finish. For many of the beautiful things in life, completeness and perfection is an illusion, a destination that we long for but may never reach. For that we should be thankful.

CHAPTER 5:
Emptiness means possibility

Emptiness which is conceptually liable to be mistaken for sheer nothingness is in fact the reservoir of infinite possibilities.
– Daisetz Teitaro Suzuki
Zen Buddhist author and practitioner

Does a mountain get lonely when there is no one to climb it?

This thought crossed my mind in July 2020 when I found out that Mount Fuji would be closed for the summer season.

The idea that no one could climb Mount Fuji in the summer season was unthinkable to me, even sad. Mount Fuji is a national, cultural and spiritual symbol of Japan. In fact, many Japanese people believe climbing Mount Fuji is a rite of passage. Some Japanese climbers have even said to me that all Japanese people must climb Mount Fuji at least once in their lives.

Mount Fuji had a special place in my heart that continued to grow the more I thought about it. I had climbed to the summit three times since 2017. I even worked in a Mount Fuji mountain hut in the summer of 2018. An empty Mount Fuji meant my former colleagues wouldn't have a job this year. Climbing tours and guides wouldn't have customers. Climbers wouldn't stand at the summit. An empty Mount Fuji meant their dreams must wait for another year.

I recalled my time working on Mount Fuji in 2018. I remembered the endless stream of climbers passing by our hut day and night. There was a lot of energy on that mountain and seeing people pursue their dreams was inspiring. I remembered some of the less desirable things of a busy climbing season. I recalled collecting broken beer bottles, crushed beer cans, cigarette butts, empty water bottles, even an empty oxygen canister during my short morning climbs up the mountain. The absence of the both the good and the bad points of working on a mountain was a painful reminder of a lost year, and a lonely Mount Fuji.

I now thought of the empty mountain trails in 2020. I thought of the mountain huts vainly waiting for new people and new memories to fill them. As I looked at all my Mount Fuji photos on my phone, I thought maybe I could send these photos and memories to Fuji to keep it company during the summer of 2020. Maybe if I was there on Fuji, I could ease its loneliness.

I imagined being on Mount Fuji in September 2020, standing on that trail that was now empty of climbers and completely clean of rubbish. I was listening and appreciating the pure, uninterrupted, natural songs of Fuji, freed from the voices of human beings. I could hear the cold autumn wind approaching, then watched it shake the mountain hut roof like a long lost friend playfully teasing the hut to wake up from its deep sleep, to open its doors so it could come inside. I could see the sparse trees along the rocky edges, comfortably wedged in the rocks to the right, swaying in the howling wind. I imagined a gale like wind exploding over the western mountain ridge, storming down the valley like an unstoppable wave, whipping up Fuji's volcanic red dust into the cool blue sky. The clouds were constantly moving, swirling around our mountain hut at 2740 meters above sea level. They settled in front of the mountain hut, shrouding it in a thick impenetrable grey mist that lingered like an unwelcome guest, annoyingly obstructing the mountain hut's view of the valley below. When the clouds kindly moved on and disappeared behind the darkening mountain ridge, the late afternoon sun re-emerged. I imagined seeing a rare complete shadow of Mount Fuji bathing the dense forest almost 1500 meters below. To me it seemed like the shadow was a blessing sent from Mount Fuji to protect the forest for the long winter season ahead.

But I wasn't really there. There were no human beings to appreciate this view – only Mount Fuji. I imagined an empty Mount Fuji, left alone to admire its own shadow and to savor its alone time. I smiled knowing Mount Fuji was enjoying a well-earned rest for the year – alone.

CHAPTER 5: EMPTINESS MEANS POSSIBILITY

MA IS EMPTINESS AND FULLNESS

For human beings, it is natural for emptiness to stir up feelings of loneliness, sometimes negative assumptions about what that emptiness means. We think an empty mountain means there is no one there to explore it, even conquer it. We think a pause in a conversation is uncomfortable empty silence that must be broken with our own voice, our own opinion. We think an empty room must be filled with things; they reinforce our sense of permanence, our identity. Emptiness confronts us with the possibility that we have done nothing; we have never achieved. For a writer, a blank white screen is bad. Writers must write something on the screen. When things are empty, we instinctively want to fill it with something. We fill it with an idea, a voice, a dream, a worry, a memory of the way things were.

On the other hand, a full mind, a full space and place can be stressful. It can seize our own space, our privacy, our time to think and breathe. A full life, packed with deadlines, responsibilities, tasks and worries, stress, agendas and biases can wreak havoc on our lives.

EMPTINESS MEANS RESET

In Chapter 3 we learned how Ma changes in time and space, how empty becomes full and full becomes empty. Zen Buddhism tells us this is the natural flow of life. Both are important. Fullness means fulfilment, the end of our journey, while emptiness allows us to dream, imagine, create, rest and reset, and begin a new journey.

Japanese Zen Buddhists believe Ma conveys a sense of emptiness in time and/or space. Emptiness is a form of retirement from the world, a space and time to be freed from our everyday cares of the world, our mental states like greed, jealousy, hatred, delusion and ignorance. Our minds need to be emptied of these states because they lead to suffering, they stop us from leading happier and more fulfilling lives. Emptiness is a restorative state of pureness that we should all seek.

Meditation empties our minds, but there are other ways in which we can create that emptiness. We can create more emptiness in our lives by cleaning our rooms and getting rid of things we no longer need in our home. In her book, *The Life-Changing Magic of Tidying Up*, Japanese author and tidying expert Mari Kondo says discarding the things in our home we no longer need declutters our lives. It helps us focus on the things that do matter and make us happy. A minimalist life is about having the right amount of fullness and emptiness in our homes and lives.

Japanese people have a saying when they walk into an empty room: *nani mo nai kukan ii* (nah-nee-moh-nah-ee-koo-kan-ee). This means there is nothing in this empty room and that is nice. An empty space or a clear room, a field and office is beautiful. Imagine coming into work early and there is no one there. It is completely quiet. You sit and enjoy a cup of coffee or tea in silence while you catch up on your emails uninterrupted. When I worked in an office full time, my favourite time of the day was when it was silent and empty.

If you don't work in an office then imagine coming home from a busy day. You have so many things on your mind. You walk into your home that you had cleaned and tidied earlier. There is nothing between the walls and the bookshelves, couches, tables and drawers at the end of the room. There are no books to move, no children's toys to put away. An empty space in between is what we long for. It is where we put our heads down, relax, breathe and let our worries float away.

DO YOU LIVE IN THE INK OR THE WHITE SPACE?

Did you notice the 2 blank pages before this page? Did you stop momentarily to glance at them or did you go straight to this page?

When human beings see an empty white space, we think something is missing. We think this white space must be filled with something right away. Some of us immediately fill this space with notes, pictures, anything to make this blank white space useful. We fill it with assumptions about why it exists and why it is a waste of time. Others flick through the pages to get back to the pages with the writing. After all, this is why many of us buy a book. It appears that for some people, life is not for living in white spaces, but rather living in the ink and the words.

Some of us on the other hand, are intrigued, even curious about these white spaces. White spaces evoke reflection. They are relaxing, calming. A book that has little white space in it, that has no pictures or no blank pages between chapters, can be exhausting for me. We need some white spaces to rest. They are an important part of our lives. White spaces can be beautiful when we stop to think about them, feel them and experience them.

CREATE MORE WHITE SPACES

Japanese calligraphy follows the spirit of Zen Buddhism, the belief that the emptiness, the white space is beautiful. The undrawn white space, the *yohaku* (pronounced yo-hah-koo), on the calligraphy canvas, where there is no black ink, is alluring. *Yohaku* is about leaving the right amount of space between the drawing and the white space. It creates balance, an energy between the white space and the ink. The more space there is, the greater the tension. This tension draws the viewer in, invites them to complete the unfinished work. *Yohaku no bi* (yo-hah-koo-no-bee) means the beauty in the white space, an invitation to complete the universe.

Where are these white spaces in daily life? White spaces are a pause in a conversation, a pause in a presentation, a short break from work. They are weekends dedicated solely to our personal lives. They are a lazy Saturday morning without doing anything productive and not feeling guilty about it. White spaces are the distance we create consciously and unconsciously between our personal lives and work lives. They are the gap between us and the office space we are walking towards, the emptiness, the final seconds of privacy we need to reset before we start our busy day. When your life seems busy and full, try adding more of those white spaces to your life.

EMPTINESS MEANS POSSIBILITY

When I moved to Japan in 2017, I was quite surprised how many rooms were 'empty', with no permanent bed. Futons are placed on the floor for sleeping and then put back into the closet the next morning. That same space can be used later in the day for studying, for having people over for dinner.

In Western society, the rooms in which we sleep are filled with something that is stable, a bed where we sleep. We fill our other rooms with furniture, pictures, awards. A filled home gives us a sense of permanence. It reminds us of our history, our family, our childhood, our successes. An empty space makes us feel unsettled, invalidated, incomplete.

I remember a friend telling me about a new home she had bought in Sydney, Australia, a few years ago. She was excited about looking at it again now that the previous owners had moved out. It was hers finally. The next day, she called me saying when she saw it without the furniture, it was no longer homely and inviting. It was barren, empty and incomplete.

Daisetz Teitaro Suzuki, renowned Zen Buddhist author and practitioner, once wrote that an unfilled space can also mean potential. Without that furniture, emptiness invites us to think how our home can reflect our own personality. How do we want that room to look? What colour will we paint our room? What bed do we put in? Emptiness can be energizing, personal and full of unlimited possibilities.

CAST OUT YOUR PROCRASTINATIONS

Emptiness is difficult to achieve. On one hand, we want a full and busy life. It makes us feel important. On the other hand, a crowded life can be bad for our well-being. When our lives are too crowded with ideas, tasks, things, this full life creates stress. This is especially true for the many tasks or projects that we put off doing. These procrastinated tasks end up accumulating to the point that we feel buried under a mountain of unfinished tasks that we want to complete but are either too busy or too fearful to finish.

Think of a person whom you had an argument with. You want to call and apologize but you hesitate. You keep putting it off because you are worried, uncertain of how that phone conversation will play out. This state of incompleteness, if unresolved can continue to nag away at us until we get it done.

It may sound counterintuitive to what I was saying earlier that incompleteness can be beautiful, but in this case, these unfinished tasks can linger in the back of our minds. A phenomenon known as the *Zeigarnik effect* assumes that we tend to forget the completed tasks but dwell on the unfinished ones. A 2017 research article in the *Journal of Occupational Health Psychology* suggests that, for some of us, unfinished tasks can make us ruminate over these tasks to the point that it negatively impacts our sleep. Observing 59 employees over 12 weeks, this study revealed that unfinished tasks can lead to increased levels of sleep impairment. What's even more interesting is that this sleep disturbance was linked to how much the participants dwelled on their unfinished tasks.

When I returned to Japan from Australia in March 2020, I had a mountain of unfinished tasks waiting for me. I thought about them day and night. I was losing sleep, and when I was awake, my mind felt overwhelmed. I needed to purge these tasks from my life.

After some deliberation, I decided to finish off those unfinished things that I put off because they were too difficult. They had been on my mind for a year. I wanted to finish them but I was either too busy or too intimidated with the mountain of unfinished tasks I had created. So, I started with the easy stuff, gained confidence and worked to the harder stuff. When I started emptying my life of such things, my stress levels decreased. So, when you are feeling overwhelmed and life seems all too much, pause, but then finish those unfinished tasks. Finish that not yet completed course, or get rid of those books you will never read that dominate your bursting-at-the-seams closet. Empty your life of your procrastinations.

KEEP BAD MA OUTSIDE THE ROOM

Ma is an empty mind that is free from our attachments and biases, the unhelpful mental states like anger and fear. If we avoid emptying ourselves of these emotions, they stick with us and can harm our relationships. Research on *excitation transfer theory* suggests that our feelings from a past encounter can carry over into our present. This means if you had an argument with someone at 1:00pm, you may carry those lingering feelings of anger into your 2:00pm meeting. Moreover, you may vent that residual anger onto that person in that 2:00pm meeting.

In his book *Before You Know It*, social psychologist John Bargh describes *excitation transfer theory* in three stages. In the first stage, we know we are angry. We can feel our sweating, our heart and pulse are racing in anger, and we know the person in front of us is causing that anger. In the second stage, when we have left that meeting, we think we have calmed down, but that anger is still there for an hour or so even though we are unaware of it. In the third stage, we are no longer angry. Research suggests that when we are unaware of our arousal like in stage 2, we may unknowingly carry this arousal into other spaces and meetings with people.

John Bargh's research suggests that lingering emotions can also affect our appraisal of the situation. We may even misattribute those lingering feelings from a past 1:00pm meeting to the people in our 2:00pm meeting. This means we may assume that the person in that 2:00pm meeting is the one who is making us angry, not the person in that 1:00pm meeting. This research suggests that lingering emotions create bad Ma between ourselves, our friends, our colleagues and family. We need to empty ourselves of these unhelpful emotions to make the Ma good again.

Think of your negative emotions as Bad Ma that needs to be left outside the room you are about to enter. Resist the urge to go into another meeting while you are still angry or stressed. Pay attention to your level of arousal and take the time to calm down. When you think you have calmed down, wait some more. Postpone your meetings to a few later hours later because you may be still aroused even though you aren't aware of it.

EMPTY YOUR ASSUMPTIONS

Emotions can come and go, but our attachment to our past and biases can be more robust and enduring. For example, we may have negative and incorrect assumptions about what a pause in a conversation might be about. Western society has been conditioned to believe that extended silence, especially during a conversation, can be uncomfortable so we reduce that discomfort by filling this empty dialogue with our assumptions and follow these assumptions with actions. I remember reading a story about how a Japanese negotiation team became silent every time their American counterparts made an offer. The Americans, uncomfortable with this silence, assumed that silence meant a rejection of their offer, and so they lowered the price every time the Japanese negotiators responded to their offer with silence.

Our assumptions come from our past experiences with silences, our beliefs and biases over what silence means. A neuroscience research study at California Institute of Technology suggests that when we are in an unfamiliar situation, we will access our hippocampus, the episodic memory of our brain, to make sense of this situation, to fill in the gaps. Drawing from our past experiences with silence, we might assume that silence means the other person is angry at us, or unhappy with something we said, because that is what happened before. Or we might think we need to speak and break this uncomfortable silence with more conversation because if we remain silent it means something is wrong with our relationship. But these assumptions from our past could be wrong.

TEST OUT THOSE ASSUMPTIONS

The best thing we should do is to stay in that silence and test out those assumptions. Had the Americans from the negotiation story waited for the Japanese to respond, they would have found out that this silence was Ma, a time and space where and when the offer was being considered and not a rejection of their offer.

When we stay in that uncomfortable empty silence a bit longer, it may turn out that silence doesn't always mean someone is angry at us or dissatisfied with our actions. Silence can be an opportunity to understand someone better. How we deal with silence can be a measure of how well we relate to each other in silence, and most of all, the quality of our relationships. An empty space of silence between us, which is free of bias and expectations, I think is a good thing. An empty and pure mind is something we should all seek.

PURIFY YOUR MIND

Have you ever wondered why Japanese people wash their hands before entering a shrine? Before they enter a shrine, they will go to a water basin called a *temizuya*, which means a place to wash hands with water. According to Japanese Shintō, sacred spaces like a shrine need to be pure, free from negative energy. Shintō religion believes we may unknowingly carry impure, negative thoughts from our lives and the outside world into this sacred space. Washing our hands is the ritual of purifying our hearts and minds of negative thoughts and energy that must be kept out of sacred spaces.

TEMIZUYA

The sumo ring is another one of those sacred spaces that must be purified of negativity and evil spirits, which can lead to misfortune or injury. One purification ritual in sumo is the *Yokozuna dohyō iri*, which is performed by a *Yokozuna*. This ritual takes place at a shrine or before a

CHAPTER 5: EMPTINESS MEANS POSSIBILITY

sumo tournament, and also during the tournament, before the elite sumo wrestler matches begin.

YOKOZUNA DOHYŌ IRI *AT SHRINE*

A Yokozuna performs a series of rituals and poses that invites a spirit, a kami to reside within them, to give them and others luck and strength. For this to happen, a Yokozuna needs a clean, pure and empty mind. If their mind and heart aren't empty of negativity then the kami or spirit is unable to enter and unable to become a shintai, a living spirit that gives them strength.

YOKOZUNA *PERFORMING SHIKO POSE*

There are other ways we can purify our mind before we enter a meeting, our homes or our workspace. Try meditation before entering a stressful meeting or a big presentation to clear your mind. You could use some self-talk: try telling yourself to go in with a pure mind. Zen practitioner and author Daisetz Teitaro Suzuki wrote that we should always enter a space with a pure beginner's mind, as if we know nothing and are open to everything.

CHOOSE YOUR WORDS WISELY

Saying nothing can also purify our minds. British philosopher, author and Zen Buddhist practitioner Alan Watts once said in the 1970s that words can get us into trouble if we aren't careful. The problem is that we like to use words, labels to explain the things that mesmerize us and even make us angry. Words make us look smart. They justify why we are angry. If used unwisely, they polarize, put us into opposing groups, make us feel we are better than others. Labels can make us feel worse.

Eckhart Tolle, author of the *Power of Now*, suggests that labelling feeds our ego. It tricks our ego, distorts what we are feeling, creates illusions around what we see. In his TED talk *30 seconds to mindfulness*, psychotherapist Phil Boissiere said that adding subjective descriptors can elicit emotional reactions. This means if we label someone as a jerk, a manipulator, an idiot, then we are likely to feel angry and tense up when we see them or even think about them. Naming, especially using verbs like gas lighting or adjectives like aggressive or manipulative, creates drama and heightens our emotions. It raises our blood pressure. Not labelling takes the negative energy out of it.

Telling someone to stop labelling others is a great idea but it doesn't come easy. Labelling is a human reaction to get closure, to get clarity, to explain why people do things, to make us believe we understand them, or so we think.

When our mind is empty of these labels, we see things the way they are, rather than what we think they are. An empty mind, free of fear, anger, distraction, and busyness is hard to achieve, but when we can attain it, we are open to filling it with things that are better for our relationships and our well-being. When we stop and observe, and resist labelling, our stories change. We are adding new twists and turns to our stories, enriching them as they unfold in front of us.

EMPTY YOUR MIND WITH NATURE

More of us are going out into nature than ever before. There is a reason for it. Nature has this magical ability to empty our minds if we stay in it long enough. When we are in the city, in the workplace, even in our homes, we are constantly busy. We study intently for an exam, we work late to finish a report, we block out all of those other things that we love to do. These tasks require enormous attention and if we do them too long, we lose our productivity, our creativity. We burn out.

Attention restoration theory, developed by Stephen and Rachel Kaplan, states that nature offers us that restorative space. It assumes that when we spend time in nature, or even look at scenes of nature like a waterfall, a mountain, a beautiful forest, our concentration improves. This is because nature requires effortless attention. It is less taxing on our minds and bodies. It redirects us involuntarily to restore our minds, so that can go back to those tasks requiring intense attention feeling more refreshed.

Recent studies show that walking in nature can also reduce our stress levels in as little as 1 hour. In a 2019 study conducted in Berlin, Germany, 63 participants would walk for 1 hour either in nature or in the city. Prior to their walks they had activity in the amygdala part of their brain measured through MRI. This area of the brain is associated with stress levels, which means that the higher the activity in the amygdala the more stressed the person is. These pre-experimental measures would be compared to their post experimental amygdala activity after their 1-hour walks.

For those who walked 1 hour in nature, MRI results revealed lower activity in the amygdala area of the brain. For those walking in the city, MRI results didn't show a decrease in the amygdala, nor did it increase. Whether in nature or in the city, going for walks can be restorative, or at least keep our stress in check.

STARE OUT INTO AN EMPTY FIELD

Emptying your mind of negativity can be as simple as sitting on a park bench, remaining silent and looking out into an empty field. I remember one August Saturday morning in 2021. I had been working inside my apartment for most of the week and so I wanted to go out. I drove into the city and walked around the near vacant streets. I walked around Kushida shrine in Fukuoka, but there were quite a few people there, so I looked for some quiet space. There, in the middle of the city was a lone park bench that overlooked a vacant field. There were no kids playing around, no one walking through the field. Maybe just a few patches of grass, but for the most part, it was empty. As I stared into this empty field, all the worries I had on my mind had magically disappeared within 10 minutes. My mind was empty, ready to be filled with something else.

FILL YOUR HEART WITH ART

After leaving that empty field, I walked by an art shop. As I turned the corner, a painting caught my eye. I froze and curiously examined it. In that painting there was a single sailboat with a sailor standing in front of the main sail, but that person's face wasn't really clear. This boat was navigating through an azure and slightly choppy sea. There behind, filling almost all of the blue sky, were cumulous clouds. Some of them were dark along their edges. Their dark blue colour to me was a sure sign that a storm was in the distance, looming somewhere behind those clouds.

As I love sailing and anything blue, I couldn't help but imagine that it was me standing on the deck of that boat, feeling the warm sun on my skin and the wind caressing my cheeks, hearing the wind rattling the full white head sail and yellow main sail. This painting mirrored my thoughts and feelings. The bright azure water was my happiness and freedom. The dark blue colour around the clouds was my sadness that there was no one to share this with. When I stopped to take this all in, I realized that I wasn't really alone.

A painting, a photo, an exhibit, any one of these transports us to another place. It creates an imagined meeting place between the viewer and artist, a space where two kindred spirits meet, where two hearts connect, where our emotions mirror each other, where we are comforted and we no longer feel alone.

Art feeds a hungry mind and weary, lonely heart that is searching for inspiration and for someone who will listen. When we stop our world and fill our heart with art, a breakthrough meeting happens. Our minds and hearts fill with beauty instead of hate, dreams instead of despair, creativity instead of limitations. Art graciously connects us with the artist, the dear friend whom we need to meet, yet will never meet, but nevertheless the friend who may understand our soul better than anyone else.

EMPTINESS IS EXTRAVAGANT

World renowned Japanese architect Arata Isozaki, known for his 1979 "MA: Space-Time in Japan" exhibit at the Cooper-Hewitt Museum New York, recently said that silence and nothingness are extravagant for him. The pause between sounds and the nothingness is Ma.

Whether we are standing on an empty mountain, gazing out into an empty field or entering an empty office, Ma tells us to stay in that emptiness and linger in silence. Wait long enough and that space will fill us with something better, something that is right for us. Emptiness can be extravagant when we pause and wait.

CHAPTER 6:

Pause and read the air

With your mind as high as Mount Fuji, you can see all things clearly. And you can see all the forces that shape events; not just the things happening to you.
— **Miyamoto Musashi**
Japanese philosopher and swordsman

Japanese Kabuki is one of the oldest forms of theatre in Japan, dating back to the Edo period (1603–1867). Kabuki is dynamic, emotional and engaging. Often actors will engage with the audience, talk with them to make it livelier. It was at a 2018 Kabuki performance in Ginza Tokyo where I learned about the art of the pause, that is a performer's ability to mesmerize the audience with silence and stillness. As I was hypnotized by this moment of stillness and silence, someone from the audience in the upper levels, screamed out:

"*Shachō!*"

Shachō in Japanese means president. Why was this person doing this as the actors were performing? Why call out president? A few minutes later, it happened again. The actor suddenly froze in his performance. Silence filled the big theatre for a few seconds before another person from the back screamed out from the top of his lungs:

"*Narita ya!*"

One of my Japanese delegates reassured me this was normal for Kabuki. It is called *kakegoe* (kah-keh-go-eh) or shouting. This often happens when an actor does a *mie* (mee-eh), a pose where they freeze to express an intense feeling or an event.

The people who call out are called *ōmukō* (oh- moo-koh) in other words, 'far away'. As the actor does this *mie* and holds it, these audience members call out the actor's family/relative group they belong to. Their shouts are meant to encourage these actors and to praise them. Some people may say, "We have been waiting for this," or "*Narita ya*", which means that person comes from a Narita family. They may even call them *Shachō* or president because the audience sees that person as dignified.

KABUKI MIE *AND* KAKEGOE

The *mie* represents a Ma, a pause between their last action and resuming that action again. For the *ōmukō*, their *kakegoe*, their shouts, must be inserted into that pause at the right time. Good timing enhances the Kabuki experience. It livens up the atmosphere, gives the Kabuki actor energy and motivation. If the shout is too early or too late then that person has bad timing. In Japan, bad timing means we are *KY*. *KY* stands for *kuki yominai*, (koo-kee-yoh-meh-nah-ee) meaning you can't read the air, or the mood or hidden meaning, or your timing is off. Being called *KY* in Japan isn't a compliment.

Since living in Japan, I have come to appreciate that the air is an invisible and untouchable vibe, a good and bad feeling we get when we enter a space and share it with the world. Without words, the air reveals when we are happy, sad, scared, in harmony or in conflict. The air tells us how to behave, how to communicate, how to live and work. It even tells how long a pause should be held and when it should be released. Yet air doesn't explicitly tell us how to do this. There is no need to. It should be obvious if we are reading the air correctly.

READING THE AIR IN JAPAN

Reading the air is important for our relationships but when we are in a hurry, we may rush into a situation, a new space without giving the air much thought, without understanding the expectations of how we should act, how we should speak. This can get us into trouble, put us at odds with everyone else, even disrupt the harmony. Stopping to read the air gives us that clarity. It tells us how to create a healthy, safe space between us.

In Japan, conversations can be indirect, vague, sometimes incomplete and it is up to the other person to read the air, to decode it. This can be difficult when no one is saying anything or doing anything and yet we are expected to know what everyone else is thinking. In Japan, reading the air is like an essential sixth sense, a silent form of communication, a social telepathy, perhaps a social barometer that is tuning in and mindreading each other's fears, concerns, unspoken desires.

VIRTUAL SPACE IS READABLE

Since 2020, many of our interactions with friends, colleagues, students had moved to a non-physical online space. Our virtual video meetings were a portal, a meeting place where people from other cities, countries and continents connected to share information, innovate, feel a sense of belonging. In this space, our ways of interacting had changed. There were new rules, new norms for how we acted in this non-physical space. People expected us to have our cameras on to show our engagement and got annoyed when people turned off their cameras. Reading the non-physical virtual space is a lot more difficult when the people aren't in front of you. Without their physical presence in front of us, it is hard to read their body language, their expectations over how we should work and live.

In August 2020, I held some probono classes on how to work remotely. I had been working remotely off and on since 2007 as a teacher and so I thought I could pass this experience onto Japanese business professionals who seemed to be struggling with working in the online space.

I had taught remote classes online through video classes, but I noticed when asking my Japanese participants questions, there was more silence between the question and the answer – more Ma. Within a few seconds of this silence, I asked them again. It didn't take long to figure out from the subtle reactions of my participants that my timing was off. I interrupted students while they were still thinking of an answer. I was in a hurry to get things moving, in a hurry to cover the material in the limited time. It turned out that I wasn't reading the air properly.

Japanese culture and psychology research provide some clues on how we can read the air better by being more patient, observing the other person's body language, focusing on the needs of others, learning to decode the silence, paying attention to our timing and being sensitive to the context we are in.

BE CONTEXT SENSITIVE

Reading the air in Kabuki means understanding the context, like when it is the right time to stand up and shout. There are also times when people refrain from shouting when a Kabuki actor freezes and does a *mie*. Cultural researcher and author Edward T. Hall, writer of *The Silent Language*, explained how Japanese culture is a high-context society. This means it is important to pay attention to the context, to the silence and to the words that are spoken before and after a word – otherwise you get the meaning wrong.

The word *shikaku* (shee-kah-koo) has many different meanings. *Shikaku* can mean a square, a blind spot, qualifications, or assassin. But they are all pronounced the same. A few years ago, I was having dinner in a teppanyaki restaurant in Nagasaki. When a Japanese guest used the word *shikaku*, I thought I heard a Japanese guest say there was an assassin in their hotel room. Of course, I knew this wasn't true, but it sounded like that. Everyone in the restaurant, including the chef, laughed. Of course, I wasn't really paying attention and didn't catch the other words before and after. What that person was saying was that their hotel room was square.

SPOT THE MICRO-EXPRESSIONS

Reading the air is the art of picking up on the unspoken words that are often expressed in people's body language and facial reactions. Our body language expressions send a message to the other person that needs to be decoded. This can be difficult if the messages we receive are very brief and conflicting.

American psychologist and professor Dr. Paul Ekman has been researching emotions and body language since 1964 and in the course of his research, he identified micro-expressions in 1967. Micro-expressions are rapid changes in body language and facial expressions that suggest an attempt to conceal something. Micro-expressions can appear in many forms. It can be smiling at someone when hearing their ideas and then rolling our eyes for a split second.

In another example, we may smile to show we agree but then for a split second, we reveal contempt through pursed lips and eyebrows lowered and drawn together. The smiling is the conscious effort to show agreement, while the pursed lips and the angry eyebrows, which appear for only a split second, are true unconscious feelings hidden behind the smile. A micro-expression can also show ambivalence. A friend could come across as being positive, but in a split second, their facial reaction switches to worry, then goes back to smiling and appearing upbeat. People who can read the air can pick up on these micro-expressions and decode their meaning.

NOTICE THE CONTRADICTIONS
A contradiction in someone's behavior is another non-verbal signal to pick up on. One example is laughing inappropriately or nervous laughter. Nervous laughter can happen after hearing a bad joke or a bad idea. In Japan, where nervous laughter is quite common, many foreign residents or visitors, who have not yet learned to decode this micro-expression, believe this laughter means agreement and enjoyment, but what it really means is discomfort or disapproval.

FOCUS ON THE SPEAKER, NOT YOU
Reading micro-expressions or contradictions takes time, practice and needs an empty mind. If we are thinking too much about ourselves, our own beliefs, then it is next to impossible to pick up on these. Focusing on others in the online space is difficult, especially if we have other distractions around us, like a kettle boiling or a dog barking in the background. In the office, we didn't have as many of

those distractions when we were in a meeting room. It is easier to be zoned into face-to-face meetings than online ones. In a face-to-face meeting, people can tell whether you are mentally in the room or not. In the online space, we have more freedom to drift in and out of these meetings, and, of course, more distractions to mentally take us out of them. This could be one of the reasons why people find it hard to be fully engaged in their remote work and in online video meetings, when our cameras are on.

In the online space, perhaps our greatest distraction is our worry about how we are being perceived. In 2020, Allison Gabriel and her associates from the University of Arizona conducted a research study about online video meetings. Their findings suggest that in video meetings, we become overly concerned with our image so much that it becomes difficult to read other people.

The point I am trying to make is to perhaps let go of our worry over how we are presenting ourselves or how well we are teaching an online class. Speaking from my own experience of teaching online in Japan for the first time, I would sometimes look for the nods and the smiles from my participants to reassure myself that they enjoyed my lesson. There were times when I would lose my concentration when I saw a confused look or someone folding their arms or appearing distracted. From my experience, we need to let go of these worries. If we don't then it's difficult to do our job properly. It's hard to read the social air when we are focusing on our private air.

OBSERVE THE AIR SPEED

We have implicit rules around how fast and how slow we want to develop our relationships and work towards a deadline. It even varies across cultures. Cross-cultural researchers and authors Fons Trompennaars and Charles Hampden-Turner found that cultures differ on the speed in which relationships are developed and business deals are completed. For Japanese negotiators, the speed in which they want to get down to business is much slower than what many foreign negotiators are used to.

When doing business in Japan, foreign companies, perhaps driven by tight deadlines, will rush Japanese companies into getting down to business and negotiations faster than the Japanese would like. In his book, *You Can Negotiate Anything*, world renowned American negotiator Herb Cohen told his story about the pace in which negotiations were done in Japan. The first 11 days weren't about negotiating. They were filled with trips to the Imperial Palace and Kyoto; studying Zen; being treated to traditional Japanese cuisine. On the 12th day, they began negotiating but then stopped and played golf. The next day, they negotiated some more but then stopped again to have his farewell dinner. On the 14th and final day, they concluded the deal just as they arrived at the airport.

While it is tempting to interpret these last-minute negotiations as a ploy by the Japanese company to pressure Herb Cohen into making generous concessions (since they knew when he was leaving Japan), I like to think this was more about Ma, how the Japanese move from the beginning of a negotiation to its conclusion. Western negotiators who are in a hurry to close the deal might see the time spent touring the country as nice but may think it is a waste of time as their deadline approaches.

For the Japanese, these non-business activities are essential. They are the bridge between the intent to enter a business relationship and the decision to consummate it. For the Japanese, business and private and social life are related. When negotiating with foreign businesspeople, Japanese people want to know the person they are dealing with first, not just the negotiator.

Japanese business people observe their counterparts on their manners, how they handle themselves in social situations, how they conduct themselves while having dinner or what they do in their spare time. Japanese people want to know how much their foreign visitors are interested in learning the culture and the language. In Japan, the process of getting to know the person is more important than the final signing of the contract.

I like to think this story has great lessons for our work and personal relationships. When we are in a hurry, stressed we may walk into a room with our expectations, our own rules about how fast or how slow we move in the space. Going into any space without stopping to read the air can lead to misunderstandings, unfavourable business results, and less than ideal relationships.

Whether you are meeting someone new in business or in a personal situation, take the time to pause, read the room and the person. Ask yourself, what are unspoken rules in this space between us? What is our relationship speed limit?

SILENCE REVEALS THE TRUTH

Strong relationships also depend on our ability to read silence correctly, but we can misread it if we are focusing too much on our own world. As a teacher, for example, I sometimes would assume that my students' silence meant they were confused, bored with my lessons. When I asked them questions and got silence, I would assume that they didn't understand the question, or they needed more clarification from me. Since writing this book, I have since revised my views around this silence. I have discovered that silence could mean my students were actually still processing that question I just asked. In that silence, they are comprehending it, refining their ideas before they give me an answer in their own time.

Silence can also mislead us, hurt our relationships if we jump to conclusions prematurely. In our personal lives, we may assume silence means our relationship is under strain or our first date isn't going well and we need to say something to save it. One person told me about his date at an Italian restaurant in Roppongi Tokyo. As he and his date were enjoying a nice Italian meal and wine, and a view overlooking Roppongi, he told me that he noticed how his date had become more silent over the last 15 minutes. She replied less and injected more of what he termed empty, white silence after he spoke. He was confused. The initial small talk and questions about why he came to Japan seemed to go well, and laughs were exchanged. She seemed interested a while ago. What happened?

He looked at his date. She smiled briefly as she was savoring her red wine. She glanced at him but said nothing. The smile was still there but became less obvious, more subtle as the dinner went on. More white silence followed. He told me how his mind started spinning. He revealed the many questions going through his head like, "*Maybe this date is going poorly? Maybe I should ask her if she thinks the date is going well. Maybe I should ask her what she thinks of me?*" As I was listening, I was thinking, NO!! Don't ask! But he did and the mood changed. There was no second date.

He gave me other scenarios, with the same pattern, with him again talking away the dinner experience, commenting how nice the dinner was, how well the date was going. More silence followed, so he talked more. While it could have been that his dates just lost interest, I thought that a lack of *Ma* could also be a factor.

In Japan, emotions are like a treasure that is hidden in that silence, and it is up to the other person to decode that silence, to understand those hidden emotions. Of course, this happens all over the world, but in Japan, silence often reveals one's true feelings if we listen and look closely. When we stay in that silence long enough, we may discover how strong our bond is, how comfortable we are with each other, how well we understand each other without having to explain it. I like to think that the health of our relationships is hidden in our conversations, but revealed in the silent air.

SILENCE HAS A NEW NAME

Research in psychotherapy suggests there are more complex meanings behind silent pauses. A 2001 research study by psychotherapy researcher Heidi Levitt identified seven categories of silence, and from that created a *Pausing Inventory Scale*. This scale has been tested and validated repeatedly over the years in therapy sessions and across cultures. According to her research, these seven categories fall under three different themes of silent pauses – productive, neutral and obstructive pauses.

FIFTEEN PAUSES | TOM FRENGOS

Productive silence

Emotional — Expressive — Reflective

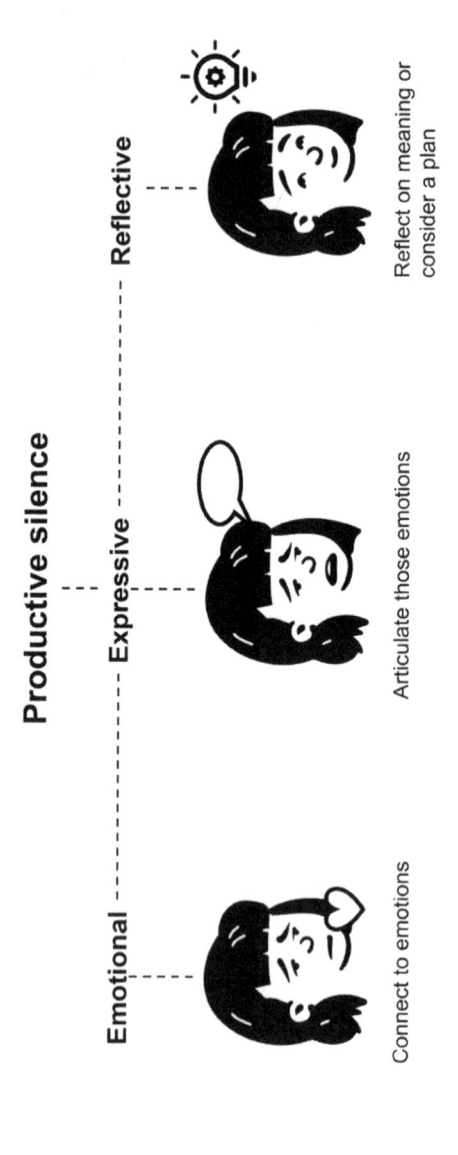

Connect to emotions | Articulate those emotions | Reflect on meaning or consider a plan

PRODUCTIVE SILENCE: ADAPTED FROM LEVITT (2001)

CHAPTER 6: PAUSE AND READ THE AIR

Productive silent pauses are emotional, expressive and reflective. Each one of these pauses opens up the dialogue between a therapist and the client, improves the quality of their relationship, and moves them forward in their therapy. For example, in therapy, clients use emotional pauses to connect with their emotions, experience them, process them. They use expressive pauses to articulate their emotions and thoughts clearly to the therapist. Clients may use a reflective pause to consider what these emotions mean and how they can use this information to move them forward in their lives. If you are a psychologist, therapist, counsellor or teacher then reading these pauses is important.

I had this breakthrough a few years ago when I was coaching a client around finding a new career. She was in a job that didn't bring her joy and was in search of a job that did. When I asked what career appealed to her the most, she paused and sat back, remaining silent as she tilted her head to the right, and looked up to think. I waited a few seconds. No reply. Hmm. Maybe I should say something? I waited a few more seconds. No response still. She then leaned forward. *Yes, she needs my advice*, I thought. I was burning with excitement to give her some advice, to recommend a teaching career, but instead I waited. By the end of the session, she'd found a few careers on her own that she wanted to explore before our next meeting. One possibility was a job in career coaching. I have since learned that a person's silence doesn't necessarily mean we should speak or give our own opinion just because we are paid to do so. Silence can be a non-verbal request from that person to let them make their own discoveries.

These forms of silence are used every day in our personal or professional lives as well. We use silence to connect with our excitement and worry about living overseas before revealing them to our close friends, colleagues and family. When we look at a once-in-a-lifetime sunset, we use silence to connect with our emotions of awe, beauty, even sadness. We become silent before we utter a word. We search for the right word to describe how viewing this sunset makes us feel beauty but also sadness because we know this moment will soon pass. We pause to reflect on what this moment means for our lives, and what we can learn from nature.

Reading and naming the silence is important to everyone. It reframes the silence we are witnessing. It encourages us to stop and listen to the other person, to remain silent when witnessing a beautiful moment instead of talking about it like human beings tend to do.

CHAPTER 6: PAUSE AND READ THE AIR

Neutral silence

Mnemonic — Recalling event, order of event

Associational — End topic or switch topics

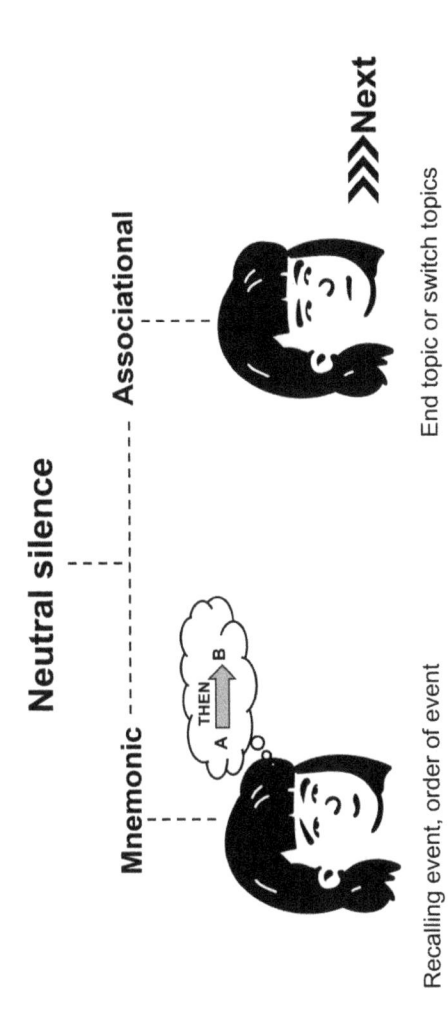

>>>Next

NEUTRAL SILENCE: ADAPTED FROM LEVITT (2001)

Neutral silent pauses are used to process information before speaking. We use mnemonic silent pauses to categorize information, to remember details and sequences of a past event.

Neutral pauses are also transitional. We use associational pauses when we finish a topic, change topics, try to switch topics or surrender the space so that the other person can talk. Imagine you and a friend are talking about where to go for dinner. You are quite excited and you are suggesting a few places to go. Your friend seems less enthusiastic. She is distracted, upset about her unsuccessful job interview today. As you make suggestions about dinner and ask for her opinion, she may pause for a few seconds. You might now think she disapproves of your choice or she is thinking about the pros and cons of that choice. What it could mean is that she wants you to finalize the dinner details so she can talk about her job interview.

CHAPTER 6: PAUSE AND READ THE AIR

Obstructive silence

Disengage — **Interactional**

Avoid emotions or end discussion

Consider PROS and CONS before speaking

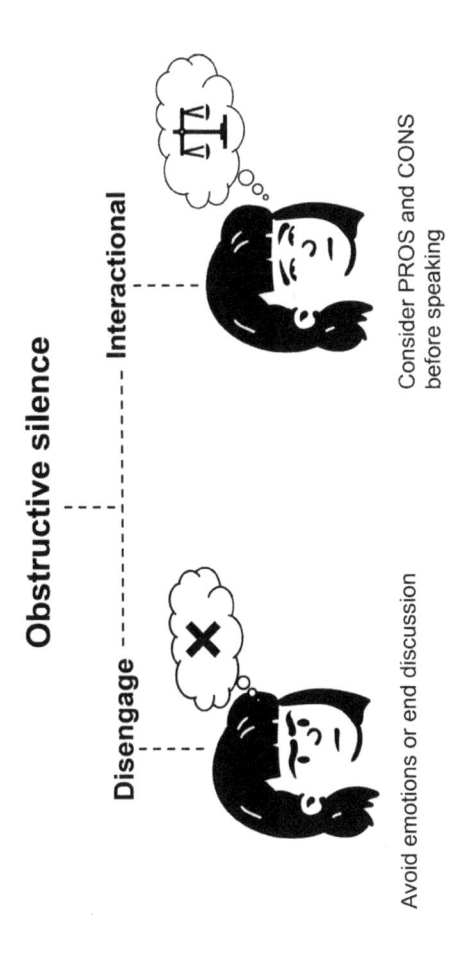

OBSTRUCTIVE SILENCE: ADAPTED FROM LEVITT (2001)

Obstructive silence, on the other hand, can disrupt the flow of communication, create distance between us. Imagine your supervisor wants your opinion about who to hire for a new role within your company. You have two candidates and she likes both of them, but you like neither and you want her to look for new candidates. Your supervisor keeps pressing you for your opinion. You avoid stating your opinion. You are hoping she will read this silent message and change the topic without having to confront you. Alternatively, you use an interactional pause. You pause to consider your next words carefully, as the wrong ones will embarrass you, perhaps even negatively impact your working relationship.

SILENCE CAN BE DECODED

How do we decode the silence? Heidi Levitt's pause research suggests that we should reflect on what happened before the pause and what happened after that. For example, if you asked someone a difficult question before that silence and that person broke their silence with a laugh, it could mean they might be trying to lighten the mood. Perhaps it means they are uncomfortable with that question and they don't wish to talk about this topic anymore. For the more obstructive pauses like withdrawing, we may need to ask that person what is behind their silent pauses, otherwise these pauses will continue to obstruct our relationships.

Remember that story about where to go for dinner? We can decode that silence by remembering our friend's disappointment about her unsuccessful job interview before she paused, and her relief later when she talked about it after we finalized the dinner details. From our analysis, we learn that her silence was her subtle hint that she wanted to shift the conversation to the interview.

UNREAD SILENCE IS SUBLIME

Reading the silence means you know when to speak, when to shout during a Kabuki performance. You know when to clap when a song ends or even when to console someone who is silently grieving. Yet, while writing this book, I have discovered there are times when silence shouldn't be decoded, read, or broken too quickly, otherwise we cheapen that human moment. Silent air, in its simplest form, can be a pure, sublime, bittersweet time – a time when we are emotionally rested between scenes, a time when we are escorted between musical notes, a time when are left alone to silently remember a departed loved one. Sublime silence isn't analysed, or described. It reminds us that there are times in life when we should accept those silent pauses for what they truly are – precious cracks in life that are best kept mysterious and unread.

CHAPTER 7:
Maai – create a graceful space

The art of life lies in a constant readjustment to our surroundings.
– **Kakuzo Okakura**
Japanese author, The Book of Tea

Readjusting is the key to healthy relationships – that's what Japanese calligraphy taught me. Every time I put my calligraphy brush on the paper, every time my hand and brush navigate around the inked words and that unoccupied white space, my narrow views of space expand and my mind ponders. In one session, I wondered what would happen if I had two Japanese words, both with strong identities, written on the same paper? Would their meaning change? Can they coexist on a small sheet of white Japanese washi paper?

CHAPTER 7: *MAAI* - CREATE A GRACEFUL SPACE

間

MA *JAPANESE* KANJI *CHARACTER*

I first drew the word Ma on the paper. Alone on this paper, Ma commanded my attention. It had presence. It radiated silence. But then I wrote another word on a separate piece of paper, *Ai*, which means to come together, to join, and to unify. This also commanded my attention. I then took out a third sheet where I would include both of them. This is where it got challenging for me. I needed to adjust the space, the size of each word so that Ma and *Ai* can coexist in harmony on this third sheet.

合
い

AI: *A JAPANESE* KANJI *CHARACTER WITH A* HIRAGANA *CHARACTER*

These Japanese words, each one comfortable with their independent existence on a sheet of paper, free to be themselves, were now meeting with one another. As I drew, I made certain that the words were equal in size, that they had the right thickness and balance so that one word didn't dominate the other. The white space on the paper now became even more sacred as I paused and scanned the space before going any further, making absolutely certain that these words were aligned with one another and separated by the right distance. Too far suggested the words were reluctant to unite with one another. Perhaps it was an arrogance that one word was better than the other, that it deserved more talking time on that paper. Too close made the space confining, so much that it prevented each word from communicating its own message freely, stopped from expressing its individual essence and spirit.

I wondered if these words could speak what would they say? Is it better to be alone on a piece of paper? Or is it nicer to be joined by another? Does this union add greater depth to their identities, expand their purpose in life? Is this beauty only possible when these two words surrender to a third word.

Japanese calligraphy, in many ways, mirrors our human need to express our individuality and seek belonging to a group. As much as we crave social contact, we also crave our own private empty space. Being in an empty space heightens our self-awareness, our individuality. It gives us the space to be ourselves. But human beings can't exist in isolation for very long, nor are we solely defined by our individuality. We are also defined by how we relate to the world, how much space we yield to others, how we behave in social contexts, how we surrender to something bigger than ourselves in a shared space. Calligraphy embodies our search for the perfect relationships, our need to get that distance and harmony right between us and the grace in the space we create when we do find it.

Since 2020, we are more aware of our personal space, more protective of it. A space can be empty but not for long. It can quickly fill up with other people, nature and objects, and it is up to us to find coexistence with these people or things entering our space. This is a human instinct yet Japanese people are more sensitive to this given that they live on an island with limited space. They even have a word for this – *Maai*.

FIFTEEN PAUSES | TOM FRENGOS

間
合
い

MAAI: HARMONIOUS MEETING IN THE WHITE SPACE

MAAI: CREATING A GRACEFUL SPACE

Maai (mah-ah-ee) means two or more people, things or objects meeting, coming together and uniting in a shared space and time. *Maai* was mostly used when talking about maintaining our optimal distance from our opponent in martial arts, but its use has since been expanded to other areas of our lives. Japanese professors believe we use *Maai* in our everyday lives, without even knowing it. Tetsuyo Kono, Professor at Rikkyo University, suggests Maai is respecting our encounters with another life in a shared space while Keio University Professor Masaki Suwa believes *Maai* is the energy and empathy created between two or more people in that meeting, reading another person's movements and intentions, making physical and/or mental adjustments of that distance so that we win in a martial arts competition, or coexist with one another.

I like to think that good *Maai* is based on good intentions, a willingness to engage, connect, collaborate, be there for another life. The calligraphy example I gave earlier suggests that optimal *Maai* is a unique form of art that two or more living entities create – an art that has a depth and a richness we can't create on our own. *Maai* is a unique, fleeting meeting that can't be repeated so we must always be prepared to adjust our *Maai*; matching whoever and/or whatever is sharing the space between us; attending mindfully to what is unfolding between us right now; noticing how our body responds; tuning into our feelings and thoughts; being in rhythm with another life.

DO WE LIKE BEING ALONE?

Before we talk about that shared rhythm, let's talk about what it means to be alone in a space. A space, without another person or another living thing to share it with evokes loneliness, sometimes even fear. Yet we also crave that empty private space, a space that is ours alone, a space to take care of ourselves, a space to entertain our own thoughts and dreams. Many of us love these alone moments when we walk into a vacant train, when we drive along an empty road, or when we drive to work alone just after dropping off our kids at school. We enjoy them when sitting in an empty park to enjoy nature, or coming into the office early before someone else does.

We need those alone spaces, that emptiness. That emptiness, according to Japanese neuroscientist, writer, and broadcaster Ken Mogi is a moment of Ma – a moment of purity. I believe these pure moments free us from our obligations. They give us permission to reset our day; they kindly remind us of who we are and what is important to us.

When we are alone, it is tempting to think that this moment defines who we are as an individual. But when a person enters our space, our world changes. We have another human being, another life to consider, another part of our identity that we, as a human being, are ethically required to express.

Japanese philosopher Watsuji Tetsurō, who lived between 1889-1960 believed that human beings have a dual purpose in their lives. One is to be an individual; to contribute to the world as an individual; to be defined by our individual actions and our personal results. Our other purpose is to be a member of society; to have a good relationship between human beings and nature; to relate to each other in an ethical way. Living that ethical life meant knowing when we are taking up too much space or seizing that space inappropriately from others and nature. Watsuji Tetsurō believed that being the total human being meant balancing our own needs with the needs of others, recalibrating that space and living harmoniously with all life we meet in that shared space between us.

In the last chapter, we learned about reading the explicit and implicit messages we send into the air, how we communicate with another human being in silence. In this chapter, I will talk about reading our movements in the space between us and how we can relate to each other better, connect, be there for each other. But first, let's think about the shift in energy that happens when another life enters our space.

NOTICE THE ENERGY

Whenever two or more people meet in the same space, there is an energy, a vibe created in that space. Each person generates their own energy, and if we watch and listen carefully, we can feel that energy. This energy might be a fascination over someone, or a curiosity over who that other person is. We can feel this curious energy in our first meetings with people whom we are physically attracted to. Think of an attraction you may have had with your partner when you first met. Was there an energy between you and that person? Was there an attraction, a feeling you couldn't put into words, an energy that stirred your need to learn more about that person, a magnetic energy that drew you in?

We notice this energy shift in our personal and professional lives, like when we meet a new person or when we walk into a new space that other people have already settled into. These people will also react when we enter their space. Being new to that space, we might be welcomed by some or viewed suspiciously by others.

Imagine walking into an office, and as you walk through the lobby you can feel the welcoming vibe, the friendliness, the way people greet you with their eyes, the way people work and collaborate. The energy in this space seems positive and inviting. Now I want you to imagine walking into another office but the vibe is different here. You get a frosty reception as you enter the lobby. The people in that office don't smile much. They seem quite serious. They whisper to each other as you walk into the room. They look away as you walk past them to find your desk, at the back corner of the office. You immediately sense the energy is different here. It is uninviting, tense, uncomfortable.

Maai is a sensitivity to the energy given off by another life when we meet in a shared space. At its worst, this meeting evokes a negative energy or bad Ma. It sparks suspicion, fear, resentment, sometimes conflict. At its best, this energy is filled with a willingness to connect deeply with that other life. As human beings, it is important we pay attention to that shift in energy when we walk into another space, or when another person enters our space.

Whenever you enter a place, a space with others, pay attention to the reception you get. Is it warm, cool or frosty? Do you feel a welcoming energy, an invitation to move closer, an openness to speak and share with another human being, with another life? If not, how can you create that trust, that welcoming energy between you? One way is to listen to your body.

LISTEN TO YOUR BODY

When I do Japanese calligraphy, I pay attention to my posture. If it's straight and relaxed, my brush strokes are fluid. When I am tense and bring a negative energy to that space, my brush strokes are bumpy, disjointed and my drawing experience is forced and not really enjoyable. The level of tension in my body also determines how I hold the brush and the pressure I put on the paper as I draw. If I am tense, I put too much pressure on the paper and my drawings seem thicker. If I am relaxed, I put less pressure on the paper and the drawings seem softer, more appealing to me and my calligraphy teacher. Since learning Japanese calligraphy, I am more aware of what my body is doing in the drawing space. I have learned to listen more to what my body is telling me, like what changes it wants me to make in my life.

Since then, I have a greater appreciation around how our body reacts in the space when we are alone and when another person is in that space with us. When someone sends us a welcoming energy, we move closer to that person welcoming us. Our body and posture feel relaxed. When we feel unwelcomed, our body tenses up, we cross our arms, we look away from that person, and if we can our body moves us away from that person. Our body reactions can determine how close or how far we want to be from them.

ARE WE AT THE RIGHT DISTANCE?

Every day, we engage each other from a physical and psychological distance. On a train, we stand physically close to one another but remain psychologically distant from one another through silence and by not directly facing that person. Facing strangers directly in such a closed space is awkward, uncomfortable. In a personal setting, being physically close suggests we welcome that person's company, and are open to being psychologically close with them.

But that isn't always possible. We can still feel welcomed, psychologically close, even when we are separated by great distances. Our video online meetings from 2020 onward proved that we didn't need to be physically close to bond with other human beings located all over the world.

CHAPTER 7: *MAAI* - CREATE A GRACEFUL SPACE

We also experienced this virtual psychological connection with our families, friends, loved ones when we couldn't be physically there.

Japanese martial arts offers us valuable lessons around optimal distance, how there are times when distancing ourselves is needed and other times when we must move closer. In aikido, karate and kendo and any other forms of martial arts, *Maai* is maintaining an appropriate distance from our opponent. As our opponent moves inward for a strike, we must back away to regain that optimal distance.

Maintaining this optimal distance can mean the difference between victory and defeat. If the opponents are too far away, it is difficult to attack. If they are too close, they are hemmed in. They are vulnerable and unable to fight back.

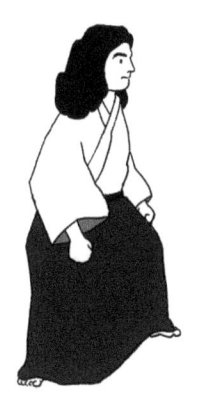

JAPANESE MARTIAL ARTS AND MAAI

ENTERING ONE'S VULNERABLE ZONE

Even when an opponent attacks, they immediately back off to regain that safe distance, otherwise their attacker can enter their vulnerable zone and strike. In karate, it is important that you measure the space between you and your opponent so that you can properly defend against their attack.

Not all of us practice martial arts so the rest of us learn from our experiences in our daily encounters with family, friends, colleagues, strangers. In daily life, the physical and psychological distance between us can suggest whether we are welcomed or unwelcomed, in harmony or in conflict. Measuring the distance between us allows us

CHAPTER 7: *MAAI* - CREATE A GRACEFUL SPACE

to appraise the person and the moment. Having a short distance between two people suggests closeness, understanding, collaboration, friendship. Close distance invites physical contract through handshaking, a pat on the shoulder, or a kiss on the cheek. Closeness can also make us feel uncomfortable if we don't ask for it or want it.

In their book *The Japanese Mind*, Roger Davies and Osamu Ikeno wrote that in Japanese samurai movies, we would see a samurai lord's loyal retainer, their assistant maintaining distance from their lord while seated. This distance is meant to show respect and hierarchy and also to give enough distance so that the other person was well beyond the length of a sword. In these ancient times, these retainers were taught to be 90 centimeters behind their lord and to be careful not to step on their lord's shadow.

SAMURAI AND RETAINER

Roger Davies and Osamu Ikeno wrote how Japanese children love to play the game called *Kage Fumi* where they would try to step on each other's shadow. In modern times, stepping on one's shadow symbolically is an infringement on one's personal space.

Speaking out against a superior is in some ways an infringement of that personal space. It means we have broken the ranks, moved ideologically closer to their senior, perhaps stepped on their shadow or cast a larger shadow of our own to dominate the space.

In schools, students are expected to maintain a healthy physical distance and an ideological distance from their lecturer. This is about respecting the hierarchy. A student who closes that space by speaking to them at close distance or disagreeing with them is a violation of that optimal distance.

However, things have changed. The online space seems to have been softened the rules and boundaries of hierarchy. Employees who would rarely get to speak to their seniors now suddenly have the chance to voice their ideas, although they still need to main to maintain some distance by not dominating the conversation. In Japanese Izakaya restaurants *Maai* is recalibrated. In these informal settings where food and drinks are involved, managers want to hear their subordinates' opinion, even if that person disagrees with them.

Distance is an important part of our daily engagements. Standing or sitting close to another person can mean friendship, intimacy. At a long distance we sense aloofness, but for others it can mean safety, a space to maintain our private thoughts, space to separate us from something we don't want to be a part of. In other words, our distance is our unconscious and conscious intent to engage or disengage from something or someone.

WHAT ARE OUR INTENTIONS?

Our intentions to bond and collaborate with another human being are reflected by how we feel, how we move and act in the space, like how we share that space or dominate it or how we try to push our agenda or our desires onto another person. If we pay close attention to the people around us, we can read their body language, their messages, their contradictions. We can read what they want to do in our meeting space, and what adjustments we might need to do to honor their intentions and ours. The key is to show that empathy for another person, to understand how they think and feel, and to remove our personal agenda out of that space.

Reading the intentions of another person means we know when to close a sale or when a junior employee is ready for a promotion. It happens in our romantic relationships as well. Even in a wordless moment, we both instinctively know when to take a relationship slow, and when it is time for us to confess our love.

Before doing anything rash, stop and observe that person's movement and their position in that space. What do their movements and distance in that space suggest? Do they want us to move closer? Do they want to enter into a relationship with us? What are our intentions? Are we here to collaborate, fight or love?

RECALIBRATE FOR OPTIMAL DISTANCE

Once we understand each other's intentions, we recalibrate the physical and psychological distance between us. It is important to know we can be at the right distance one moment, but then that distance may be inappropriate later on. In martial arts, the same opponent may show a different move from a different angle and we must therefore adjust our distance from that person. In our personal relationships, our partner or child may enter the room feeling happy one day and sad the next. In that case, we may need to offer more physical contact to our loved ones, to comfort them, to listen to them without judgement, to show them we are there for them.

It takes special sensitivity to know the situation has changed and to know to what degree we need to adjust our distance. Think of a working relationship between you and another colleague that has gone bad. One moment you are comfortable sharing your ideas. You are speaking openly without judgment. Then suddenly that connection is lost. You argue with one another, you feel hurried into sharing your thoughts or feelings about a topic you aren't prepared to discuss now. Like in martial arts, you restore that distance by moving back to your desk, or leaving the room.

Yet there are times when we can't create physical distance between us, when we can't walk away. Instead, we use silence to create that distance. In the book *Silence and Silencing in Psychoanalysis*, clinical psychologist Aleksandar Dimitrijević wrote that silence can be a form of resistance. We may become silent because don't want to share our thoughts our feelings. We want to protect ourselves, keep our thoughts private, avoid saying something we will regret later on. Whether we are a friend, a teacher, a coach or psychologist, it is important that we read these changes in the air, the silence that enters the space. Once we read it, we can adjust by accepting the silence, asking fewer personal questions, changing the topic and slowing down the pace of the conversation. As discussed in the previous chapter, a pause of silence can mean a request for more space, a request to change topics, or to slow down the pace in which our relationships are developing.

Good optimal *Maai* means we are processing this information consciously and unconsciously to adjust our space and actions. We use this information every day to keep safe, to grow our relationships, to collaborate with others, to learn and to love, and be in harmony with one another.

FOCUS ON HARMONY

Japan is a small country with limited space. Citizens and residents of Japan live in a world with crowded trains, busy train stations and long lines of people waiting patiently in front of restaurants during lunch time. When I pass through the bustling stations of Shinjuku or Shibuya or

Tokyo station and try to board a jam-packed train during rush hour, it surprises me how few disagreements or brawls there are, which is almost certainly something I would see in other countries.

This need for harmony is deeply rooted in Shintō religion, which believes that all living things, even inanimate objects like a rock, a mountain, a tree have the potential for a spirit or a *kami* to enter them, so they need to be respected when we enter their space or when it enters ours. The tea ceremony also attempts to create that harmony, where people from different backgrounds, statuses and ideologies can coexist in the same small space through a shared, powerful, humbling experience.

We create these harmonious meetings by giving each other enough space to think and feel comfortable with expressing a different view. We see this when a manager allows her team to express their opposing views in a safe forum that sparks creativity and belonging. Cultural anthropologist Edward Hall, who researched Ma, suggested that *Maai* is about being present, tuning in to all objects and living things within a shared space and uniting to form a single body, mind, heart, and spirit.

AM I MAKING MYSELF TOO IMPORTANT?

Our interactions with each other aren't always harmonious. There are times when we are out of sync, not aligned with each other, even fearful of each other. Sometimes we will back away, argue, dominate a conversation, rush people

CHAPTER 7: *MAAI* - CREATE A GRACEFUL SPACE

into signing a contract, pressure people into making difficult decisions they aren't ready for, manipulate people into agreeing with us or ask others to give us feedback when they want to keep it a secret.

When we enter a space, we may have preconceived ideas as to what happens in that space and the role we and other people play in it. As a counsellor or coach, we may enter a client session with an agenda over what the session will look like, what techniques we will use, how the client will feel by the end of the session, what goals they will achieve by the end of it. As a teacher, we plan how the session will go, how our students will learn and what they will learn by the end of it. When we operate from these preconceived notions, we either consciously or unconsciously make ourselves the hero, the person who we think is the only one who can make things happen.

Pausing reminds us of this imbalance, the bad Ma that our ego is creating in that room even though it's invisible. Healthy confidence in our abilities to help and influence others is a worthy pursuit, so long as it doesn't dominate the space. It is a good reality check when we ask ourselves if we are making ourselves more important than we really are. What would happen if we let others take the main role on stage? What if we stopped trying to control the outcome and, instead, surrender to what is emerging between us and allow ourselves to become part of something bigger than ourselves?

HUMBLY SURRENDER

At the beginning of this chapter, we learned how individual Japanese *kanji* characters have their own personal meaning, but when put on the same page with another one, the meaning in that space is different. The same thing happens with human beings and other lifeforms. When we are working for a company, the company purpose isn't defined by our personal meaning but rather a shared meaning that we all try to embrace, a meaning that transcends our personal interests, our own ego. This can be difficult because following a goal that is not solely ours has us wondering if we are surrendering our individualism, our power. Surrendering requires a strong dose of humility, the belief that our individual needs are less important than the needs of something greater.

Sumo wrestlers are one of the humblest athletes I can think of. When a sumo wrestler wins a match or even beats a high ranked player like the *Yokozuna* (the highest ranked sumo wrestler), you rarely see them scream in jubilation, and you rarely see them scowl when they lose. Showing such emotions on the *dohyō* (the ring) suggests a lack of restraint and disrespect to the sumo gods.

There have, however, been times when a losing sumo wrestler had to be called back to the ring to bow again because the referee felt that the sumo wrestler did not show proper respect to the victor. Even when they are interviewed, the victor speaks quite humbly, as if winning was not a big deal and it was just a match.

Sumo wrestlers rarely use their family name when competing. Many will use a ring name, their *shikona*. Sumo wrestlers do not always choose their *shikona*. Sometimes their trainer may choose it and it might be based on where they train. Recently retired Georgian sumo wrestler Levan Gorgadze also used his ring name, Tochinoshin Tsuyoshi. Tochinoshin's name comes from his fighting stable *Tochi*, which is the Kasugano *heya* (training stable).

Most sumo wrestlers live in communal training stables, where strict sumo tradition dictates what they eat, how they dress and how they behave inside and outside the sumo ring. In 2013, three sumo wrestlers were disciplined by their stable master for breaking curfew and wearing street clothes instead of their mandatory kimono.

MANDATORY SUMO KIMONO

Not using our name of birth, withholding our enthusiasm and following strict rules to many would mean giving up our freedom, our choices on how we live, how we celebrate and who we are. But sacrificing our own interests, our own ego can also mean that we are just a person that is part of a group, a calling, a sport and a legacy. For sumo wrestlers, this humility is the soul of a sumo wrestler.

SEEK COMMONALITY AND ALIGNMENT

Sumo shows how each wrestler's contributions to the sumo tradition are more important than their personal goals. We can also see that alignment between two different ideologies which, at first, seem very different and irreconcilable. One thing that comes to mind is the commonality shared between Shintō and Zen Buddhism.

When I arrived in Japan, I wondered why Japan has two different religions. How do Buddhism and Shintō religion coexist? Japanese Shintō religion was the established religion when Buddhism was first introduced into Japan from China in the 6th century. At first glance, they seem different, but when we look for commonality, it becomes easier to integrate the two.

Shintō strives for the harmony of opposites while Japanese Zen Buddhism makes it happen. In Zen Buddhism, fixed ideas mean we will never change. When we keep them fixed, we must follow them, and biases can result. This creates disharmony. The Zen Buddhism values of emptiness and selflessness tell us not to remain attached to fixed ideas or actions. Ideas change and fade into nothingness. Biases and identity dissolve into nothingness. When we let go of these attachments, we become open to new ideas and harmony results. Buddhism is the Middle Way that awakens the magic and mysterious powers of Shintō religion.

CREATE GRACE IN THE SPACE

When there is that commonality, when our egos are silent, there is the possibility that something special is about to happen between us. We see this when two or more people are working or performing together, in synch with one another, creating a form of art that can't be created by one performer alone. In August 2018, I witnessed this art in a Japanese Kabuki theatre. One of the more dynamic scenes I remember was the changing of costumes on stage, while the actors were still performing. As the main actor was performing, there was a *koken* (or stage assistant) crouching down, shadowing the actor, staying behind them, following them as they performed. When the actor stopped, the *koken* started pulling on a thread that was attached to the actor's costume until their top costume disappeared and their costume underneath magically appeared. It surprised everyone, including me. It transformed the atmosphere. It livened the mood. For such transformations to work, the actor and the *koken* need to read the music, read each other's movements, wait for the tension to reach its peak, when the audience is ready for that grace in the space.

HIKINUKI: *REVEALING THE COSTUME UNDERNEATH*

We can see this in other parts of the world as well, like in Spanish flamenco, where the dancer changes their steps as the guitarist changes their beat and the singer raises and intensifies their voice. In this space and moment, we know what the other person is thinking. Even without speaking to each other, we know what the other wants and we know what to do. We are comfortable with each other in those moments of silence, those pauses, and moments of uncertainty. A space of grace is filled with the silent communication between us, the empathy we feel and the respect we give for each other in that once-in-a-lifetime moment.

REMEMBER *ICHIGO-ICHIE*: ONE MOMENT, ONE MEETING
Anyone who practices Japanese calligraphy can tell you that no matter how hard they try, the characters they draw are always different. Even if they use the same technique, the same brush, the same paper, the same amount of ink, there is always something different about it, subtle differences we may not notice right away. Calligraphy is a unique union between a brush, the ink, the paper, the hand, heart and mind of the artist – all meeting together in harmony on a piece of paper, and no matter how much we try to replicate that meeting, the outcome will always be different.

Our unique meetings are also happening in our lives, in our real encounters with other people, animals, and nature. The meeting spaces between us are always changing and can never be replicated. I believe that in any meeting with another person we should remember *ichigo-ichie*. These Japanese words mean a "one time one meeting". Each experience, each meeting with people is rare and needs to be treasured because that moment can't be repeated – even if we meet that same person, at the same time of day, in the same room and talk about the same topic. There is always something different in that meeting. We could be in a different mood. We may have new insights, new knowledge that we didn't have in our previous meetings with friends, colleagues, family.

It is human nature to think that we may get a second chance to right a wrong, to showcase our ability in an interview, to apologize to someone we offended through our words, to tell someone we love them. But that second chance may not happen. We may never see that person again or our actions can't be erased. *Ichigo-ichie* reminds us of that. If we know we have only one chance to make a good impression, to leave a nice memory from that meeting, then perhaps we will treasure those meetings more.

When meeting someone for the first time, do your best to prepare for that meeting as if you will never meet again. If you are preparing dinner for your friends or family, put all of your heart and effort into preparing for that dinner. Think carefully about the ingredients you will use. Slow down and take your time preparing that meal. Put love into it.

If you are meeting someone at work for the first time, listen, show kindness and show that person respect. Try your best to hold that urge to dominate the space or judge the other person. Overlook the differences and imperfections each of you have. Pause and create a beautiful, graceful legacy of that meeting as if you will never meet again.

CHAPTER 8:
Open your space for change

Walls have ears, sliding doors have eyes.
– Japanese proverb

Nature is all around us. For me, there's no need to travel great distances or spend large sums of money to enjoy and learn from nature. All I need is an open window.

It was a hot September day, the wind had picked up strength, just enough to provide us with some relief from the unseasonal hot weather in Fukuoka. I hoped opening the windows would bring more of that relief into my home. As I opened my windows at the front and back of my apartment, a cool breeze immediately entered; my hallway became a wind tunnel – generously delivering that much needed cool air, aromas of blooming flowers, and sounds of birds chirping.

I then opened up my Japanese sliding doors. As I did this, my window drapes fluttered, more like danced like an over eager dancer who hadn't danced for years, now suddenly being granted the freedom to dance again. Yet the wind wasn't done with my apartment just yet. It circled around my kitchen as I was preparing dinner, flapping the papers of my cooking book, as if it was curiously checking out what I was cooking. Perhaps satisfied with my choice, it decided to move on and toss around my work papers that were once nicely stacked on my desk but now scattered all over the floor.

As I observed the wind make it itself comfortable in my home, it was becoming obvious to me how opening my windows, opening my sliding doors created a third space, a brief moment where nature and I had a conversation, where life embraced both of us and spoke. I wondered when does life decide when we should open and close our sliding doors to the world?

OPEN OR CLOSE THE SPACE?

We open our spaces, our sliding doors, every day when we speak our mind, share our feelings, let others talk freely, let more people into our world. An open space creates good Ma. It slows life down. It graciously gives us time for our creativity to flourish; it encourages us to be open minded to other ideas and show empathy towards others. Yet, some of us are hesitant to open our spaces too much. We fear that opening our space creates conflict, takes aways our power, leaves us open to criticism, ridicule, even pain. This chapter talks about one of the great

CHAPTER 8: OPEN YOUR SPACE FOR CHANGE

dilemmas human beings and other living things face. *Do we open or close our space?*

FUSUMA: SLIDING DOORS

Traditional Japanese architecture, specifically sliding doors, offers us great advice around opening our spaces. *Fusuma* (foo-soo-mah) are Japanese vertical rectangular paper or wood panels, which can slide from side to side. They act as doors, divide rooms to create intimate closed spaces for intimate gatherings, tea ceremonies, private business meanings. In these closed spaces we feel safe, comfortable, rejuvenated.

FUSUMA SLIDING DOORS CLOSED

Fusumas can be opened, even removed if you need to accommodate more people. If there is a large gathering and you need two rooms, you need to remove the *fusuma*. Removing the *fusuma* changes the entire experience. It brings larger groups together, allows more air to circulate. *Fusuma* embodies Ma. Meaning and form of a space can change over time as sliding doors are opened and closed.

In October 2019, I was watching the Rugby World Cup quarter final between Japan and South Africa. Friends from Australia had come to visit us. We decided to watch the match while having dinner but the sliding doors blocked our view so I removed the panels of these sliding doors. The room suddenly transformed from a quiet space I slept in to a raucous place to enjoy a dinner and drinks with friends, to enjoy the once-in-a-lifetime moment where Japan reached the quarter finals. This new space was full of energy and new life.

LET NATURE IN

When we think of Japanese teahouses, we think of intimate closed spaces, spaces to connect with others, liminal in-between spaces to break away from our everyday lives, spaces to forget, spaces to ponder life. Japanese architect Kengo Kuma has designed many of these closed space teahouses in the past, but for one Vancouver teahouse, he wanted to break with Japanese cultural tradition. He wondered what would happen if he opened the teahouse

CHAPTER 8: OPEN YOUR SPACE FOR CHANGE

as far as he could, open it up to Vancouver's wild natural environment.

This Japanese teahouse sits on the terrace of the 19th floor of Shaw Tower in Alberni Street in Vancouver, Canada. Overlooking the downtown district and Coal Harbour Bay, this teahouse embodies the essence of Japanese culture. It has simple *tatami* floors, a *shōji* or translucent sliding window. This teahouse is quite spacious and there is no permanent furniture within the site. When a tea ceremony is held, an accordion-like table is raised from the floor to accommodate tea ceremony guests. When it is done, the table is folded back into the floor, returning the room to its original empty state. It radiates the spirit of Ma.

At night, when the lights are on, the teahouse shines like a beacon, inviting us to come in. By having sliding doors, the teahouse can open up and guests can see the beautiful bay and mountains in the distance. The open doors create a transparency, where light, the smell of local wood and nature are invited into the building. The *engawa*, the boarded floor that runs along the outside of this teahouse, acts as bridge. It connects us with nature and makes us feel one with it.

In Japanese architecture, opening the space creates new experiences for the people living and working in that space. It transforms the space into a new reality, creating new rules as to what happens in that space, and who we can become in that space.

When we pause in Japanese architecture, our mind opens up. A building is more than just something we admire, live and work in. It is also a reflective space to imagine what the architects, engineers and builders had in mind when they built it.

Das Kranzbach Meditation House in Germany, designed by Kengo Kuma, echoes his message to open our minds to nature, to see nature not as separate to us, but connected to us. Located deep in the Black Forest in Bavaria, this building has large windows that invite nature into the building. As the sun moves across the sky and reflects off the window, it looks as if the forest is entering the building. If we stay in the space, we can see and sense the forest moving through the building, transforming every part of the space within it. The building is becoming part of nature. Nature is becoming part of the building. We are becoming part of nature.

EMPATHY NEEDS OPEN SPACES

Opening our windows and sliding doors to nature inspires us to change the way we live and work with others, to open our space to different ideas we may resist at first. This is especially difficult when we are locked in conflict, stuck in a win-lose space. We need to create an alternative space, one that encourages us to keep our spaces open even though we want to close them.

Ritual peacebuilding takes place in symbolic open spaces, liminal in-between spaces of Ma where the rules of relating are different from normal life. In Atalia Omer, R. Scott Appleby and David Little's book, *The Oxford Handbook of Religion, Conflict, and Peacebuilding*, the authors suggest that opening the space between disputing parties can lead to creativity and healing. Inexperienced peacekeepers or mediators try to limit the space around what is comfortable. They keep the space narrow, and confined to nice agreeable conversations. They control the dialogue, keep the peace when two sides are engaged in a heated argument. It's difficult to show empathy in such a closed space.

BRAVELY HOLD THAT EMPATHY

Listening opens the space. We pause, we listen, we let others say something. We surrender our space. We feel empathy for the other person. Then it becomes heated, awkward, uncomfortable. We want to defend ourselves, close our spaces but instead, we bravely keep them open.

William Ury, negotiating expert and co-author of the best-selling book *Getting to Yes: Negotiating Agreement Without Giving In*, says that listening opens the space for negotiation. It allows both sides to be heard. In his TED talk, *The Power of Listening*, he describes his negotiations with President Chavez of Venezuela. He was being shouted at by the president, with no chance to speak. Many of us in similar situations would shout back, defend ourselves, call this person a bully, take to social media and humiliate them. William Ury listened instead. He was tempted to defend himself but instead of arguing with the president, he kept listening and nodding as Chavez shouted, allowing the president to continue shouting for 30 minutes! When president Chavez finally stopped shouting, William Ury noticed the president's shoulders sag and his voice become weary. For him, that was the "sign of a human mind opening to listening".

When we open the space and listen, people feel we care what they have to say. It validates their world. This gesture encourages them to open their space and hear our side. Opening our space transforms a divisive space between us into a human space.

OPENING THE SPACE IS NICE, BUT....

In our world, we are encouraged to open our spaces, to turn our video cameras on, to put ourselves out there, to speak up and 'be vulnerable'. Society tells us that if we open up our space to the world, we will be popular, successful, have a more fulfilling life. Some of us are okay with letting people into our private world. We even admire those who courageously share their private world with us. In the online space in 2020, we saw videos of high-powered executives delivering a speech while their 5-year-old daughter unexpectedly came screaming into the room. It showed a humorous, human side to people we never saw before. Opening the space seemed like an attractive option in a world that was closing down.

Earlier we learned that *fusumas* are the sliding doors of our hearts and minds. We close them for intimacy, for privacy, for safety, for rest. We open them for learning, for love, for freedom, for new experiences. Unfortunately, these days, not everyone wants to open their sliding doors so freely.

When I was running online workshops around the topic about working remotely, a few students spoke about feeling pressured to have their cameras on during their video meetings at work. Another student told me of her experience as an online delegate, how she became annoyed when the facilitator asked her to turn on her camera to introduce herself as soon as she entered the online meeting. Once she introduced herself and the discussion went back to the facilitator, she proudly told me how she turned off her camera right away and said nothing else for the remainder of that meeting.

OPENING UP IS EXHAUSTING

Research suggests opening ourselves to the world with our cameras on can be uncomfortable and exhausting. A research study conducted by Allison Gabriel and her associates from the University of Arizona revealed that having the camera on can induce fatigue and potentially lead to less engagement and participation. With 103 participants and 1,400 observations over a 4-week period, Allison Gabriel and her team found out participants experienced more fatigue when they had their camera on than when they had their camera off.

Their research suggested that Self-Presentation Theory could explain this. Self-Presentation Theory assumes that we are driven by a need to be seen in a favourable light and so we try to give positive information about ourselves. This means we focus on how we appear and how we are behaving in these meetings. Being able to see our own video image on the screen means we are evaluating ourselves more than we do in face-to-face encounters. This puts a lot of pressure on us because we feel that we are being watched and evaluated. It prompts us to manage our image, which can lead to fatigue. We put on a smile to show we are engaged when we actually may be tired or bored. No wonder people feel hesitant to keep their cameras on.

DO IT ON YOUR OWN TERMS

Being asked to turn our cameras on when we would rather keep them off goes against our basic need to freely choose. When we feel we have no personal choice but to open our spaces, to put ourselves in the spotlight, we feel as if we are giving up our privacy, our values, selling out to someone else's narrative that we should be all be transparent and crave being in the spotlight.

Self-Determination Theory, developed by Edward Deci and Richard Ryan, suggests that we are driven by a need to freely choose to do something that is enjoyable and has value to us. Doing enjoyable things keeps us engaged, makes us more competent and happier. When we feel forced to open our spaces, like keeping our camera on, we feel frustrated, anxious and resentful for doing it. We become disengaged and participate in these online meetings half-heartedly.

Richard DeCharms' theory of Perceived Locus of Causality Theory (PLOC) claims that our actions are motivated by external or internal benefits. This theory suggests that even though we are reluctant to have our camera on, we turn it on because it gives us money, recognition, rewards. Yet not everyone turns on their camera for money or rewards. Some of us do it because it wins us social approval. We turn on our camera because we feel we *should* do it; it is the right thing to do as a team member, as a fellow human being. Doing things for social approval, to connect to something more important than ourselves might work in the beginning, but over time, we start to wonder if we are ignoring our own needs.

Some of us find value in turning our cameras on. We think we *could* turn on the camera, because it appeals to our values like our need to bond with others. Some of us turn our camera because we *want to*, because talking with other people is fun and enjoyable. It engages us and is an expression of our true selves.

Not all of us will want to turn on the camera for too long, or even at all. Yet there will be times when some of us want to share our feelings, connect with people across great distances. Find those times and who knows? Opening our spaces may not be so bad after all.

SHŌJI: HINTS WE ARE READY

Some people are reluctant to open their world. They may still want to do it, but are being held back by the fear of being taken advantage of, looking weak or unprofessional. Opening the space, in this case, is done subtly and it is up to the other person to pick up on these signs and to create a space where the other person feels comfortable opening up.

Shōji (shoh-oo-gee) is a Japanese wooden lattice structure with paper affixed to it. Unlike the *fusuma*, which is opaque, *shōji* is translucent, allowing light to come through. In the daytime, a *shōji* lets the daylight come in. It brightens the room, and its mood. At night, when the interior lights are on, it gives a glowing quality. From the outside, we see shadows moving. We sense something is happening. It arouses our curiosity and invites us to imagine what is happening.

The shadows and light we see in a *shōji* are a lot like people who want to open up to us, but need to do it subtly. People may desire to share and open up, but fear that opening up completely means they will be hurt. Subtle hints, like the shadows in a *shōji* window, suggest their desire to open up, but also a hesitancy. Their body language, their tone of voice, their contradictory messages – all of these are a sign they may want to open up. As a coach and teacher, my job is to read these subtle messages by paying attention to sound of their voice, their body language. Are they leaning forward to show a willingness to open up? Is their voice more upbeat? Are they smiling? All of these are hints that they want to open their space and hearts to us.

SHŌJI SLIDING DOORS

So how do we create these *shōji* conditions? How do we encourage people to open up gradually, subtly and how do we read it? One way is to fill the space with kindness or positivity, through humour, faith and patience for people to open up in their own time. When people feel safe, unhurried and supported with this light, and feel they won't be judged, they are more willing to open up their space.

WAIT FOR THE MAGIC

Opening the space comes in many different forms. It is the symbolic opening and closing of a window or a sliding door. It happens when we expand the space, when we allow people to talk and create, when we listen even though we want to keep talking. It happens when we move from a narrow space of self-focus to a more open empathic, other-focused human space.

Opening the space is difficult for some of us. We want to open up but are too preoccupied with our own world, our agenda, our own power. Some of us fear opening the space means people will take advantage of us. Some of us do it slowly. While others just need a little nudge. All it takes is to watch, listen, and wait for the magic, the subtle sound and sight of a human being opening their heart.

PART III:
Existential pauses – who am I becoming?

CHAPTER 9:
Be friends with the void

Mysteries of mysteries, water and air are right there before us in the sea. Every time I view the sea, I feel a calming sense of security, as if I am visiting my ancestral home. I embark on a voyage of seeing.
– **Hiroshi Sugimoto**
Japanese architect, photographer

Looking out to the empty ocean awakens our human instinct to explore. For centuries we have crossed the vast ocean void, searching for new lands, new beginnings, a new life. These oceans, which have existed since the beginning of time, will continue to humble and inspire us until the end of it.

In his video interview *Hiroshi Sugimoto: between sea and sky*, Hiroshi Sugimoto described how the ocean was the birthplace of his consciousness when he was a young child. During a family vacation, on the return journey between Atami and Odawara, his train passed through a tunnel on a cliff and when it emerged, a panoramic view of an empty Pacific Ocean and cloudless sky appeared before him. At the sight of this, he realized "I am here and I exist."

The memory of that ocean inspired him to travel around the world, to stand on cliffs and photograph the sea day and night – searching for that perfect ocean without boats, clouds, sunsets or sunrises. In 1980, when he was taking photos of the Caribbean Sea from the Jamaican coastline, he had a breakthrough. On most days, there were "dynamic cloud formations" but, on that day, those clouds were gone and the sea was empty. It was a mirror image of the ocean he saw in his youth – a rare vision that became his first photo of his Seascape series.

His Seascape series, all monochrome photos, show equal balance between the sea and the sky. The sea horizon is placed dead centre in the middle, so that air and water is captured in equal halves, to show balance. When we look deeply into these photos, we see what Hiroshi Sugimoto sees. Reality bends, space and time become boundless. We travel back in time to a pure, unspoilt ocean that existed centuries ago, an ancient time when human beings first became conscious of their existence as they looked out into the sea. In these oceans, these empty seas, where time is only measured by night and day, where time transcends our short existence, an infinite sea horizon immortalizes us.

Like looking out into an infinite ocean, we have our own voids. We become stuck in them, stay in them, explore them, become self-aware in them. We then begin to think of how to fill these voids and how to cross them. Our 'oceans' are bittersweet voids we need to face, our inner journeys we take towards a new beginning.

WE ALL EXPERIENCE VOIDS

We all feel voids at some point in our lives. We feel a void when we lose our job, when we retire. We feel it when our children leave home or when we realize we will have no children to pass on our legacy. We feel it when a loved one passes away, or when a relationship ends. A void evokes feelings of absence. We feel the loss of our past, a loss of joy, companionship, purpose.

A void steals our dreams, traps us, humbles us, separates us from others. In times of transition, we may feel an existential void, unsure of who we are – that we have no identity. We feel alone in a still, vast and open sea with no past to define us and no future to inspire us. We are unsure of how to get back, which way to swim. When we pause in this void, and stop trying to swim somewhere, it becomes clearer to us that our journey to filling this void with something or someone will happen – when life decides we are ready.

LIVING IN THE VOID

Anthropologist Victor Turner's influential twentieth-century research on ritual process of the Ndembu people of Zambia suggests that moving from our regular lives into a liminal world is disorienting, unfamiliar, even void-like. But once we get settled in, we ultimately anchor into this world. We form social connections. We establish new norms and behaviours in this space and time. We create a new normal. Sailors who spend months at sea, create an everyday life in this void. They have customs, rituals, social connections, jobs to do. It gives them purpose and belonging. They develop their sea legs.

During 2020, we looked to find ways to fill that void, to occupy our time, to distract us from what was happening in the world. We were playing games or social networking on the internet, creating funny videos of dogs complaining about self-quarantine life. We were watching movies and doing video conference calls. All of these were novel and effective ways to fill this void. Some people were taking sake sommelier courses, learning knitting, making art, or creating music and videos to express themselves, to connect with others. This was our new normal.

A VOID IS BITTERSWEET

Earlier we learned how emptiness means new beginnings, multiple possibilities. A void is different. We feel a loss of something – a hole in our hearts. It's so uncomfortable and painful that we want to fill that void immediately to ease that pain. When we end a relationship, we begin a new journey to finding a new partner to fill that void, believing this will make us feel whole again and make us happy.

Pausing and waiting in a void is a bitter space. We want to break out of this void, this silence, this inaction, this loneliness. Yet, if we break out of it too early, we may miss things, important things. We forget to ask ourselves what we want, what the world wants from us, what our hearts want to say. When we forget to pause in the void, we make the same mistakes over and over again.

AN UNCOMFORTABLE VOID

When we pause in the void, contemplate in it, listen to it and speak to it, we learn new things. We can fill that void with something or someone else. We fill it with our feelings, our creativity, with new meaning, with new friends.

PAUSING IN A VOID

DOING NOTHING IS BORING

Research suggests that human beings dislike void-like conditions so much that we look to stimulate ourselves externally. We may even prefer feeling pain over doing nothing. In a research study at the University of Virginia, led by Timothy Wilson, participants were asked to sit alone in a room for 6 to 15 minutes with no cell phone, and with nothing to read or nothing to write. They were asked to do nothing but to let their minds wander or daydream. Most participants didn't enjoy this experience. They found it hard to concentrate. However, when participants were put into an empty room with a phone or reading materials, it was more enjoyable and easier to concentrate.

Later, these participants were put into the same conditions, but with one added twist. There was a green button they could press to administer themselves a mild uncomfortable electric shock, which they had been earlier exposed to prior to going into the room so they knew it was painful. The research revealed that for those in the empty room, two thirds of male participants and one quarter of female participants gave themselves the shock while in this empty room. It appears that when some of us are sitting in a room, with nothing to do in this void, administering pain to ourselves is better than doing nothing.

Research suggests that we would rather be stimulating ourselves externally with the internet, speaking to others, exercising than the alternative. We assume that being in void-like spaces, without that stimulation, without action is boring, a waste of time. And yet emerging research suggests it might not be as bad as we think. A recent study from Kochi University of Technology in Japan and the University of Reading in the UK reveals that when we are told we will be put in a room to just think and do nothing else, we will assume it will be boring. But when participants from Japan and the UK were asked how engaged they were after the study, the waiting activity wasn't as boring as they predicted.

MEDITATE IN A VOID

Meditation can evoke void-like feelings. That might be the reason why some people dislike meditation the first time they try it. When we sit in a meditative pose in silence, we aren't stimulating ourselves with conversation, texting, or reading. This change can disorient our brains as we cope with this absence but soon, we are forced to pay attention to our thoughts, our senses that we often ignore in our daily busy lives.

We may dislike at first the senses and thoughts that are filling these void-like spaces. Our minds may fill with worries about the world we left behind, unfinished tasks that must be done immediately, unchecked emails that must be answered. As we settle into meditation, in this void, we become more aware of our bodily sensations like the tension in our bodies, the aches and pains in our knees. We become more aware of our breathing which some people may find unpleasant. Yet, if we sit in this void long enough, we begin to see that void may not be empty or bad. It is filling with new sensations, new feelings, new thoughts, new worlds.

EMBRACE NOTHINGNESS

During 2020, I thought of William Bridges's three stages of a transitional journey from his book *Transitions: Making Sense of Life's Changes*. The first stage is endings, where we leave our old world behind. We separate ourselves from our normal lives and move into a neutral zone, a void of uncertainty, anxiety, disorientation, a loss of self. Awaiting us at the end is the third stage, a new beginning, a new world.

In any time of transition, whether we are between careers, waiting for the results of a medical test or an exam we took, we are moving from one shore to the other, through this neutral zone, this void. But this void can make us feel stuck, like we aren't moving nowhere. Yet the void, like the ocean, can inspire us, if we could stop and sit in this void in our lives and reflect what it means for us. Before we reach that new beginning, that new shore, there is still more to discover, more to learn in this void.

Japanese architecture creates void like spaces for visitors to pause in that space more, to contemplate what is missing and to discover the beauty of the void. Japanese architects like Kengo Kuma and Tadao Ando create these voids through large high ceilings or by creating holes in the building to let light come through. When I walk through such buildings, I often look up at the high ceiling with a sense of freedom and also a sense of awe. I am left humbled by the sheer size of this building. It reminds me how small I really am and how I am part of a bigger world.

The Water/Glass House located in Atami, an onsen town in Shizuoka Prefecture, also has this void-like effect. Designed by Kengo Kuma, this guest house uses glass windows and floors that create an illusion that the guest house is dissolving. From some angles, it appears as if the building, the ocean and the sky have merged into one single entity.

Buildings such as these create the illusion that the building has disappeared and nature only remains. This sense of loss of the material of a building encourages us to contemplate, abandon our need for objects, for material things. We understand why nature is so important, why we need to merge with it, find harmony with it, and why it makes us feel good.

LISTEN TO YOUR VOID

Kengo Kuma says that "in traditional Japanese space, the most important space is the void or space Ma." In a video interview for the Royal Academy exhibition *Sensing Spaces: Architecture Reimagined*, Kengo Kuma said that we "work with the void to feel something."

I believe that void also speaks to us. It enters our mind, with uncomfortable thoughts at first but, over time we are no longer ignoring the void nor fighting it. Our mind, heart and spirit are open and ready to listen to it, perhaps even have a conversation with it.

A void is a psychological and emotional emptiness that is invisible to the naked eye, but felt from the heart. Some of us know what our void is and have little difficulty expressing those feelings. For others, it isn't so clear. We feel something is missing from our lives, but we find it hard to express what it is. In this void, we could ask ourselves: what are these feelings and thoughts telling us? Why should we stay in this void? What can we ask it?

We feel this void when we imagine an empty office that used to be filled with our colleagues working side by side with us. We may feel an important part of who we are and where we belong is gone. At the same time, we can fill that void by mentally replaying the scenes and memories formed in that space. Playing these thoughts and visions in our minds reminds us how much we miss it, and why.

SPEAK TO IT WITH ALL YOUR HEART

As I was pondering what to write for this chapter, I was feeling empty. After remaining positive for more than a year during the *Great Pause*, I found myself in an emotional void of my own. I thought of the people lost, the livelihoods lost, what the world lost. I re-evaluated what I was doing during this time. I was locked into a writing frenzy trying to get two books done to the point that I reached micro-burnout. I suddenly lost my love for writing. For a few days, there was no meaning, no point to write, no love in writing. Writing had been my way of staying focused, remaining positive during this time, but when I couldn't write, these void-like feelings came, and they came hard.

From 2020-2021, many of us were experiencing these void-like feelings. Actually, there is word for it: languishing. This word, made popular by psychologist Corey Keyes in the mid 2000s, defines languishing as the void between happiness and depression. When we are languishing, we lose our well-being, our joy, our sense of purpose. We feel stuck, even though we try to move forward in this void. Social psychologist Adam Grant, author of *Think Again*, describes languishing as "feelings of stagnation, looking at life through a foggy windshield." I like to think of languishing as walking towards a foggy horizon in a desert, with no clear skies or civilization in sight, even though you know those clear skies are coming and that civilization will appear.

Adam Grant suggests that we can work with this void, even be friends with it, by first naming our feelings about being in this state of languishing. As I thought about this more, I was suddenly inspired to write these thoughts and feelings. As I wrote, I lost track of time. I kept writing and when I was done, an hour had passed by. When I read my writing, I was surprised to see how it expressed from all of my heart, the sadness and emptiness I felt as I reflected on the year and what we had all lost.

AS IF TALKING TO A FRIEND

While writing this book, I discovered that retreating into the void of darkness, without any external stimulation, can be restorative, illuminating. In November 2021, I visited a teahouse located in front of Nagoya castle. By the time I arrived, the sun had passed over this teahouse, and the teahouse was losing its light and filling with shadows.

As I stepped into this empty, darkening room, I was welcomed by a darkness that mirrored my own, a time in my life when I was lost in my career, a time when I didn't know what the future held for me, my family and for the world. I sat there hoping I could find some answers but they didn't come as quickly as I hoped. Yet as I sat in this room longer, one clear thought emerged. The life and career that I thought was dazzling during my younger years no longer inspired me – that life no longer existed. From the moment I left that room, I pondered what new life was waiting for me at the end of this pause, a life that honoured who I was now becoming during my journey.

Junichiro Tanizaki, author of *In Praise of Shadows*, beautifully described why we should explore the darkness even when there is no light. He wrote:

> If light is scarce then light is scarce; we will immerse ourselves in the darkness and there discover its own particular beauty.

In a space and time where we think there's nothing, only darkness, perhaps we could try seeing this void as an invitation to play and be creative, to experiment, to collaborate, to dream again. Some voids may never be completely filled, or even partially filled. Yet for some people, the void we thought could never be filled can spawn a new relationship, a new passion, a new life purpose.

The next time you meet an unfriendly looking void, pause, listen to it, speak to it. Who knows? You may become friends with it.

CHAPTER 10:
Michiyuki – journey in stillness

Along this road goes no one, this autumn eve.
– **Matsuo Bashō**
17th century Japanese haiku poem master

It was September 2021 and I was struggling to find an introduction for this chapter. I searched everywhere for inspiration. I read books, watched movies, went climbing, but that inspiration wasn't there. It turned out that inspiration was waiting for me – on an escalator step.

It was October 2021 and I was in Hakata city in search of a book just after lunch and there were, surprisingly, not many people in the mall. I took the escalator to the 8th floor, waiting patiently on the non-passing side of the escalator, while some young Japanese women with their shopping bags in tow, hurried up the passing side of the escalator. For those shoppers who weren't moving, they were oblivious to the world. Their eyes were locked on their phones, their fingers moving about frantically on their phone screens.

I scanned around me, listening to the soft music playing over the PA system, curiously looking at the shops appearing to the left and right of the escalator. As my escalator moved me towards the third floor, I looked back with regret at the second floor fading out of sight, taking one last look at the camera store and the art shop next to it. I wondered if maybe I should have stopped there and bought something.

I looked upwards towards the third floor, expecting to see something, but there were only people and steps in front of me. I felt this childish excitement growing within me, wondering what this escalator would reveal, what I would see on that next floor, what I could buy. I wanted to rush up the steps, to get to that third floor faster than the escalator was designed to go but I waited instead, with great reluctance.

As I waited on the escalator, I noticed a few people walking up the escalator, rather quickly. There was one young man dressed in a dark blue suit and sharp gold tie, flanked by an older gentleman, dressed in a more conservative looking blue suit, looking at his watch and motioning the young gentleman to hurry. Maybe I should rush up as well? There is nothing to do on this escalator. Still, I remained where I was.

Someone once told me you can tell where people are in their lives by how they ride an escalator. Those with plenty of time, who want to stay in the present, patiently wait. Some of us text on our phones to pass the time. And then there are others who walk quickly up the escalators. Thinking about this story now, I realize that many of us were and still are rushing up the escalator in life. Perhaps we rush up because we think standing on an escalator step is a waste of time, that it doesn't bring us money or achievements, that it doesn't get us to that store quickly, that it delays us from moving onto the next task, that it prolongs our journey. We want to fill our time with something more interesting and more productive than standing on an escalator.

Escalators are a form of Ma. They are a pause and we want to rush out of it. We can't go backwards and we can't always see the next floor right away. Staying still leaves us with regret for missed opportunities, for things not bought, for clothes not tried on, for jobs not taken, for conversations not had. On escalators we wonder, even worry, about a future that we are unable to see. On escalators we compare ourselves to others, watch what they are doing. We painfully watch how fast they are going up the passing side of the escalator, how fast they are progressing and succeeding in life and moving towards the future, while we stand still, underachieve and do nothing, or so we think.

The escalators of life remind us that we are always moving, maybe not at the pace we want, but still moving. In Japanese theatre, this is called *michiyuki*, our moving selves in a journey.

In the previous chapter, we learned how the loss of a career, a loved one, our health, our way of life can evoke void like feelings, confusion over what we do next in our lives, confusion over who we are. A void can set us off on a journey to filling that void. This chapter discusses our movement through that in-between space, the journey to filling and crossing that void, the journey to healing and finding that new life.

MICHIYUKI: A JOURNEY

In her presentation, *Designing Mindfulness*, Dr. Yoko Kawai defines *michiyuki* (mee-chee-yoo-kee) as a journey, "the space you covered when travelling and the time spent". *Michiyuki* has strong roots in Japanese Noh theatre and Kabuki. In Noh theatre, *michiyuki* is a prologue that is described by a priest. In Kabuki theatre, *michiyuki* often occurs in the last act of a play. It is a travel song that is sung by star-crossed lovers while moving. Both of these are meant to show our long journeys in that in-between space.

As we journeyed through 2020, we felt stuck, like we weren't moving at all, that nothing was happening in our lives. We weren't moving towards a normal life. I compared this state to the feeling of being in the middle of an ocean, with no land in sight, being motionless. *Michiyuki* is a faith that we are all moving even though we are unable to see it or feel it.

In her presentation, Dr. Yoko Kawai says that in water, we can't be still as the water is always in motion. Like being in the water, I like to think that we all face different currents every day. The currents of the world and the currents of our lives are moving as well, moving us in different directions, taking us backward in our journey, returning us to our past to remember what we left behind. They pull us forward to imagine the future, longing for that future that is still out of sight. *Michiyuki* is the wisdom to know when we need to surrender to the currents of nature and let it decide where we are going and when we will arrive.

MOVING STILLNESS AND ZEN GARDENS

Even when we are physically still in one place, our senses are moving to interpret our environment. Our mind is moving to fill that stillness we are in. We fill this stillness with memories, with fears and hopes. Even when we try to stand still, we notice that our body is still moving. Our leg and back muscles are working hard to keep us balanced, to keep us from falling, trying their best to keep us as still as best they can. I noticed this sensation when I was standing alone in a museum exhibition room in Nagasaki, how my body was moving in stillness, and how we and the world are always moving.

Dr. Yoko Kawai suggests that Zen gardens show that movement. They put us in a mindful state. At first glance, we see a still garden. As we look closer, we see that the gravel represents the ocean, the water currents, a ripple in the water. Zen gardens metaphorically show us that movement. We use our own thoughts to continue that movement. We follow the lines and circles drawn in the Zen garden sand. They give us the illusion that movement is happening in the space we once thought was still. Zen gardens are a stillness of the body and movement of the heart and spirit. In Ma, we are moving towards a place, a destination of enlightenment and healing. We are discovering new things, new passions, new careers even in a pause. We are transforming and moving in the process even if we don't notice it right away.

ZEN GARDEN

TIME TRAVEL TO THE PAST

The void in Ma, this neutral zone, can heal us when we stop and make peace with it, live with it. But how long can we stay in this void, this space of stillness and emptiness? Ultimately our human instinct to start moving kicks in again. In the summer of 2020, we wanted more. We wanted out of this void. Many of us wanted to race out of it and go back to our past. It was much better. People who were separated from their friends and family, lost their connection with others and their sense of belonging. When we couldn't move forward and see our loved ones, when we couldn't find that belonging, we time-travelled back to the past to comfort us in the present.

NOSTALGIC PAUSES

In June 2020, as I was running through a deserted track, deep in a forest in southern Japan, my mind time travelled back to 2016. There I was running the 2016 Kangaroo Island Marathon in Flinders National Park, South Australia. Everything was going smoothly until I hit the marathoner's wall at 32 kilometers. I felt excruciating pain on the sides of my knees. I felt exhausted, defeated but I kept running.

In this marathon of only 60 runners there was no one there to encourage me, no one to push me. It was just me, the wall, the doubt and the pain. My mind raced to the finish line, beating my personal best, receiving my medal, sinking to the ground in relief. My mind returned to the race, the 32 kilometer point. The pain returned.

At 34 kilometers, the strong winter wind that was whipping my unprotected face suddenly disappeared. When I reached the top of another hill, I looked around. There was no wildlife. No kangaroos! I stopped to take it in. There was nothing much I thought. It was just me and the silence of nature, an empty undulating boundless road, away from civilization, all alone, with no end in sight it seemed. I felt free.

I started running again with a sense of confusion and joy. I wanted to get to that finish line, to beat my personal best and yet, I wanted this moment to last forever.

A few minutes after crossing that finish line, as I was stretching, and admiring my finisher's medal, I thought about the pain, the doubt, the loneliness and joy at 34 kilometers. I realized at that moment I became a marathoner, that I could do anything.

I returned to 2020 to the forest, fondly remembering this story, feeling confident that I could complete this marathon we and the world were running through.

POSITIVE EMOTIONS FROM NOSTALGIA

When we are unable to move forward in our journeys, we can still time travel to the past to find moments of joy, success and failure in the midst of adversity. Research by Constantine Sedikides, Joost Leunissen and Tim Wildschut from the University of Southampton suggests that thinking of the past releases feelings of nostalgia that comfort us, reminds us how we conquered adversity before. The past gives us meaning, a resilience to work through the present, a renewed confidence to move forward into the future.

NOSTALGIC INSPIRATION: LOOKING FORWARD

Nostalgic pauses can happen when we listen to music or watch movies from our past, something that reminds us of our youth and our happy times. It can even generate positive emotions. Research from the positive psychology field suggests that these positive emotions can build resilience, buffer the negative impact from the negative emotions we feel when facing adversity. A nostalgic pause is finding that crack, that light in the darkness and staying in it for as long as we can.

LET GO OF THE PAST

A nostalgic pause works well for long journeys of healing, and career changes. But nostalgia can also work against us. It keeps us in the past, opens up old wounds, stop us from moving forward. William Bridges's three-stage model suggests that long journeys can be a source of transformation, but only when we let go of our old lives and move towards a new one.

Letting go of our past may involve a ritual, something symbolic that expresses our sadness for letting go. Yet, there are times when there are no rituals, no preparation to leave our old world behind. Leaving our old world can also be done rather frantically, and suddenly with no time to express how we feel. In our sudden departures from our old world, we may unknowingly carry with us lingering feelings of loss.

DISCOVERY EMERGES IN THE PAUSE

What happens when we feel we aren't gaining any ground in our journey? Ma can create an illusion that there is nothing in a pause. We see only two gates and nothing in between. We think there is no better option, no better life, nothing else to learn by waiting. There is no need to open the space, no need to stop and listen to what other people are saying. There is no need to change.

Emptiness and nothingness spur us to go back to our original point, our old lives, our own opinions. Alternatively, we race further ahead blindly to the end gate without any preparation or thought. It is human nature to break a long pause, quite understandable to go back to the only life we know. Yet if we just wait, and accept the pace in which life takes us, we will make new discoveries about ourselves and the people around us. Discoveries await us in this Ma, this journey, not the end of it.

ILLUSIONS IN MA: RACING BETWEEN THE GATES

STILLNESS IS A QUIET POWER

Every day, we move between silence and noise, between action and inaction. Yet, for human beings, being completely still and silent is uncomfortable if we do it for too long. People think staying still, remaining silent means we are doing nothing, we are satisfied with the status quo, willing to accept an average life, willing to let others dominate a conversation, willing to let others control our actions. In the workplace, there is a belief that doing nothing means we aren't being engaged, we aren't contributing, we aren't achieving, nor meeting our KPIs.

When we remain silent and still, people underestimate our ability, our value to an organization, even society. Inaction is highly undervalued in today's world. We think inaction equates to incompetence, lack of ambition, insecurity, weakness, passivity and failure.

Yet silence and inaction, can be a quiet power, an energy we feel as we ready ourselves to contribute to the world. At work, silence and inaction means we are thinking carefully. We are giving the solution respect rather than mindlessly and quickly blurting out a solution, just for the sake of looking like a contributor.

EMPATHY IS A JOURNEY

Our 24/7 society conditions us to believe that stillness means doing nothing but if you go to a Japanese Noh theatre performance and watch their mastery of stillness, you might think otherwise. Zeami Motokiyo, the 14th century actor, playwright and perhaps the father of Noh theatre, wrote that doing nothing in a Noh theatre performance is the most satisfying part of the performance for the audience. Like the Kabuki *mie* from Chapter 6, there are moments in a play when the main actor may suddenly stop their singing, their dance, their movements to highlight a key moment. In Kabuki, that silence is broken by the *ōmukō* in the audience shouting words of encouragement. In Noh theatre, that stillness and silence is maintained longer and it isn't broken by the audience. It is the actor who breaks that silence and stillness when the moment is right. This pause is called *Senu hima*.

Senu hima is Ma, the interval between stopping and restarting the dance and dialogue. When the action stops in Noh theatre, the emotions are just starting and a shared empathy is being released into the theatre. In Noh theatre, the actor puts great effort into holding his pause by remaining silent and trying conceal that tension as that pause is being held. This tension opens up the theatre. It creates an empathic meeting space and moment between the performer and the audience, when the audience is emotionally moved by that tension, when they feel what the actor feels, when the actor and audience share one soul.

CHAPTER 10: *MICHIYUKI* - JOURNEY IN STILLNESS

SENU HIMA (STILLNESS) IN NOH THEATRE

Shared empathy in moments of silence and stillness happens every day – in our conversations with colleagues, friends and family. Let's imagine you have a friend who is upset because she didn't get the job that she dreamed of having. You listen to her story and sense her disappointment. Then she stops talking, but she is still upset. Her face looks downcast, her shoulders drop, her face tilts downward as the reality and disappointment sink in. You want to say something, tell her that she will get another job, a better one, but instead, you remain silent and let those emotions unfold in that moment of silence.

Like we learned in Chapter 6, when a person stops talking, the emotions are beginning to unfold. They are being released, waiting to be processed. When we see our family, friends and clients struggle, we want to ease that pain. We want to tell them we are listening and we care. Emotions are like a bell we strike and the soothing hum that continues after we strike it. Like that hum, emotions resonate but then begin to slowly fade away. We need to remain silent until those emotions fade out, give that person time to process those emotions before we say something. In that silence, as our friend processes her emotions, we may feel that same level of disappointment as if we were our friend.

Rikkyo University Professor Tetsuya Kono suggests that Ma is a state of readiness, a movement towards the future, a chance to prepare ourselves for an event that is about to happen. When I teach this concept to my counseling and coaching students, I stress the importance of remaining silent and quiet. As coaches, teachers, counsellors, loved ones, we think that offering words of support will move them forward, but it doesn't always. If we break that silence too early, before those emotions fade out, that person might think we are uninterested in what they have to say, that we creating distance between us, that we don't care enough to share that pain and disappointment they feel. In our conversations, silence is a shared journey of emotions that move, settle and fade, connects us more than words can.

CHAPTER 10: *MICHIYUKI* - JOURNEY IN STILLNESS

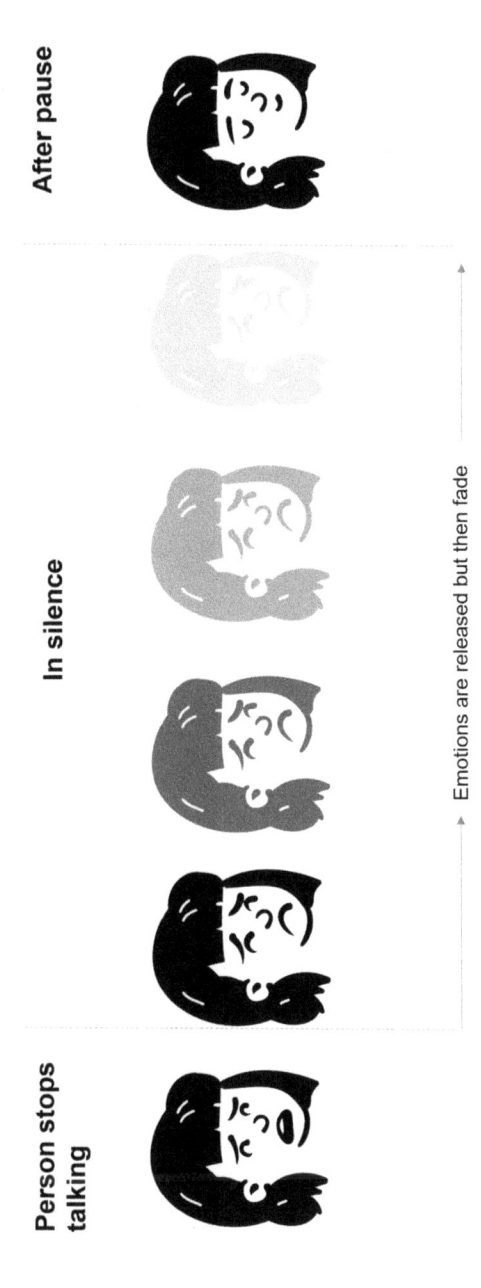

After pause

In silence

Emotions are released but then fade

Person stops talking

EMOTIONAL RESONANCE: ADAPTED FROM LEVITT (2001)

EMBRACE UNCERTAINTY

All journeys have that element of uncertainty that excite us and, at times, frustrate us. In Chapter 4, we learned that when the future is uncertain, our mind time travels forward to create a more certain future. We plan a pathway to take us to a best-case arrival and prepare for a worse one to reduce its impact. Ultimately, we realize that being the fortune teller doesn't help. It rushes us to a future we aren't yet ready for. We ignore a present we can learn from. We dismiss the mysterious pathway and take the quicker and most travelled one. As much as we need clarity in a journey, *michiyuki* reminds us that all long journeys are made in relative darkness, no matter how much we plan and prepare for the future. *Michiyuki* is our beautiful, mysterious journey.

Japanese gardens mimic this mystery, where the end is hidden from where we start. In these gardens, there are many twists and turns that are mostly hidden from our line of sight, concealed by gardens or turns that we must scan and navigate around. Walking through these gardens remind us that when we focus on our present, the future we desire pleasantly surprises us, as it begins to take on form in due time.

WALK THE *SANDŌ* PATH

Most approaches to a Japanese shrine embody that *michiyuki*, the need to be 'here and not there.' One shrine that comes to mind for me is Fujiyoshida Sengen Shrine that is located in the Yamanashi prefecture side of Mount Fuji. It rests on the northern base of Mount Fuji, at around 850 meters above sea level. For traditional climbers, this shrine is a special starting point to climb Mount Fuji. Many traditional climbers to Mount Fuji say you have not climbed Mount Fuji unless you start from Fujiyoshida Sengen Shrine.

Getting to this shrine is a journey in itself. You need to walk up hill from Mt Fuji Station and that takes up to 20 minutes. You then must pass through the first gate, a ten-meter tori gate. From here, on a clear day, you can see Mount Fuji towering above you like a god.

After going through that gate, you must cross a main road to reach another tori gate. This space is even more sacred. Behind this gate is a *sandō*, the worshipper's path that connects the gate to the shrine. This path is a long gravel pathway flanked by stone statues and tall cedar trees on each side. At first, the shrine is barely visible, as it is hidden by the cedar trees. As you walk along this path, the shrine slowly comes into view. This pathway, for many, may seem too long, even a waste of time to walk, especially if you are in hurry to finish it or want to conserve your energy for the next day of climbing. But if you go deeper, you can feel the spirit of Mount Fuji and hunger for that journey up the mountain.

I remember walking this *sandō* path to the Fujiyoshida Sengen Shrine in 2018, the day before starting my summer job on Mount Fuji. As I went deeper into this path, I found myself focusing on the sounds of the birds singing merrily, the grinding of my hiking boots against the gravel pathway. I remember the soothing sound of the cedar trees rocking in the wind that cooled my sweating body as it swept in from the north. The *sandō* slowly brought me deeper into the world of Mount Fuji, while my own world faded behind.

Walking the *sandō* path to shrines symbolizes our *michiyuki* and the speed and the way in which we walk it. Some of us rush through this *sandō*, while others go only half away because they have limited time. There are some of us who mindfully enjoy walking the *sandō* rather than reaching the shrine. Shrines like this encourage us to slow down and enjoy the *sandōs* of life, which are different for each one of us and which we must complete alone in our own time.

CREATE YOUR OWN *MICHIYUKI*

Michiyuki awakens our need for uniqueness. We love to think that even in a shared journey like living overseas in Japan, or walking El Camino pilgrimage, or running in a marathon, that our journeys are unique. Sharing a common journey is nice, but going through it faster, taking a few side roads or stopovers adds a unique feel to our journey. It creates a spiritual road less travelled within that physical road most travelled.

One thing I learned while working on Mount Fuji in 2018 was that everyone wanted to be part of the Fuji experience, but they also wanted to have their own unique story. It was July 6, 2018 on Mount Fuji, and the sky was overcast with dark, thick, menacing god-like clouds. Our first typhoon was coming to Mount Fuji. Yet, in spite of this impending storm, many climbers came. All of them were committed to getting to the top and back before Fuji would be closed off for a day.

The descending route wouldn't be open until July 10, due to lingering ice and snow on the peak. All climbers had to climb up and down via the ascending Yoshida route, creating bottlenecks all the way to and from the top. It took longer for most people and a few people weren't happy when I told them how long their journeys would take.

I remember two young climbers, quite tall, long-legged and fit looking, both wearing flashy green climbing jackets arriving at our mountain hut. They paused at the entrance, standing proudly as if announcing that they were here to conquer Fuji and everyone else had to get out of their way. As soon as they walked in, they immediately picked up their menus. Within a dozen seconds, they ordered two ramen. As they impatiently waited for their ramen to arrive, they kept looking at their watches. They checked their phones, and searched for the bus schedule to go back to Tokyo via the 5th station. They seemed quite proud of their progress so far. Most people need 2 hours to get from the 5th station (the main starting point for most climbers) to here. They did it in 70 minutes.

As they received their ramen, I overhead them talking about getting back to the 5th station by 6:00pm. It was already 11:30am! Their estimates, I thought, were wishful thinking.

As I moved closer to the table, the female climber slid her now empty ramen bowl to her left. She then looked at me seriously and asked, "How long do you think it will take to get to the top from here?"

I happily replied, "Hmm. Most people do it in 4 hours. It depends on the traffic. The trail is packed today because the typhoon will soon be here."

She became annoyed and raised her deep voice, "You don't know me! You don't know us, what shape we are in, how we have experience walking 30 kilometers in one day, in mountain terrain!"

I smiled and, without blinking, leaned inward and asked in a curious tone, "Hmm…what time would be good for you then?"

A bit surprised by my cheekiness, she gave me a half-hearted smile and replied, "We can do it in 3. No problem."

"Good luck," I said with a disbelieving, wry grin.

Four hours had passed since my meeting with that ambitious climbing pair. I then looked outside and saw them passing our hut on their return journey. I remembered that female climber smiling at me as she and her partner zoomed past me. She took one last look at me, perhaps giving me a "told you we could do it" smile.

CHAPTER 10: *MICHIYUKI* - JOURNEY IN STILLNESS

On Fuji, some people break their trip up over 3 days, others do it in 2. For the ambitious person, some do it in half a day. In our journeys, we decide how fast we go, where we stop, where we rest, what routes we take and who we meet along the way. We decide whether we should keep going or whether we should stop to have ramen before we continue. Our journeys are all different, even if we take the same physical path. *Michiyuki* is the inner and outer journey of movement and stillness we complete alone, and only we can fully understand.

CHAPTER 11:
Suki Ma – take a deep breath

Unfinished work, a gap, is an opportunity, a space to breathe, to think, to dream.
– **Japanese proverb**

Our private space is our inner oasis. It clears our minds, frees us from our obligations. We need it to feel human.

A private space can appear in many forms. It is an empty room, a deep breath, a stairwell, the edge of a long boardroom table with no one sitting next to us. It is a song that transports us to a past that only we can visit and only we can truly appreciate. Our private space is a walk in the park or a three-second pause before we speak. My private space opened up under a tree, as I listened to the songs of Japanese cicadas.

It was August 10, 2021. I was awoken by the screams of the *kuma zemis* (called bear cicadas) living merrily in the tree in front of my balcony. *Kuma zemis* are the perfect weather forecaster. You can tell how hot and humid a summer day in Japan will be by how early in the day they start screaming and how loud they are. If they started around 4:30am and their screams were quite loud by 5:30am, then I am confident to say the day would be a scorcher.

Kuma zemis are one of the loudest cicadas in Japan. On a normal day, their screams can reach nearly 94 decibels, which is the sound level of a lawn mower. But today, with all of them screaming in unison, their sounds seemed louder to me, closer to the sound levels of a rock concert – which is 120 decibels. Even with the window closed, the air conditioning on, the sound, I thought was unbearable. How can I sleep through this, work through this later this morning? I wished these cicadas could just stop for a few minutes and give me some silence.

I left my apartment hoping to escape this noise. Perhaps a drive to a nearby park would be give me that break. I walked towards my car, feeling pity for it, because it was sizzling in the relentless heat with no breeze to offer it temporary relief. It was one of the hottest days of the Fukuoka summer. The temperature reached 36°C with a humidity that made it seem like 43°C. I then turned to my tree in front of our balcony, where the cicadas were screaming. I walked underneath the windless tree and stayed there. All around me there were what sounded like high-pitched screams of agony, so loud, I couldn't hear any cars, or any people. Nothing else in the world existed but their screams. As I listened more, I realized they weren't screaming. They were singing.

It's hard to understand what the cicadas are singing when you are looking for words. When you stop looking for words and keep your mind silent, you can temporarily live the life of a cicada. Cicadas live a short life once they emerge from underground where they live for nearly 2 years. Cicadas sing endlessly throughout the day and there is a reason for it. They are looking to mate and have a short time to do it because they will die within a week. It seemed only natural that I would be moved by their fragile songs that sit somewhere between the brief, narrow, sad boundaries of life and death. For one moment, as I stood under this tree, I was in a private bubble, totally forgetting my worries, the heat, the noise. The cicadas had become my private space, my escape from it all – they were my *suki Ma*.

SUKI MA: A BREATHING SPACE

A *suki Ma* (soo-kee-mah) is Japanese word for a crack, a gap, an opening in a time and space. I heard the word *suki Ma* in July 2020 from a Japanese friend who worked as a marketing manager for a Japanese firm. A *suki Ma* for him meant a niche market, a business opportunity that no other company had yet to find. I learned later in 2020, that a *suki Ma* is important in our everyday lives.

A *suki Ma* is a break in the clouds, a chance to go out for a run after three consecutive days of rain before the rain returns once again. For other people, *suki Mas* are bittersweet spaces we find levity in moments of despair, surprising times when a hopeful light kisses the darkness and promises us everything will be okay – and we believe it. These spaces are our personal sanctuaries that appear out of nowhere, close up quickly and maybe gone forever if we wait too long.

Not all of these *suki Mas* are fleeting. They can be more permanent, like a small alley in the back of a restaurant you work at, where you take a break after a long busy dinner. It can be a small corner of an office that you can retreat to when you want a break from crowds and people. These spaces can be a personal claim for privacy, even power, like where a contractor secures their hot-desk seat in an office before someone else gets it.

A *suki Ma* is a private space like a vacant room or the faraway corner in a room where we calm down after a huge argument. It can be the space outside a meeting room, where we give ourselves encouraging self-talk before we go inside to deliver a big presentation. It is the hallway we walk down, as we gather our thoughts, clear our minds, before we start a big sporting match. It is a moment of silence when we retreat to our own private thoughts and remember someone we have lost.

A *suki Ma* is an opening in a conversation when someone has stopped talking and we can jump in and say something. When a person stops talking, we think perhaps that person has left something unsaid but what it really means is that we are invited to enter that open space and to continue the dialogue.

Some Japanese people say *suki Ma* is the opening in the darkness. We need these openings to create private spaces from work, to take a break, to think before acting, to get that fresh air. Without these spaces, without these time-outs, we feel breathless and confined. We feel emotionally, intellectually and spiritually stagnant.

LIFE ALWAYS HAS OPENINGS

In December 2020, I contacted a calligraphy teacher to draw up twelve Japanese characters that I could use for another book I was writing. I watched as she slowly, purposely and delicately painted these twelve characters.

The calligraphy teacher finished the Ma character, then placed it delicately on the floor at the back of the room for me to look at. I looked carefully at this character. I noticed some parts seemed unfinished. They had a crack, an opening in them.

CALLIGRAPHY TEACHER'S MA

CHAPTER 11: *SUKI MA* - TAKE A DEEP BREATH

It was this unfinished part in the teacher's Ma, the openings that had energy, that sparked my interest. I showed my teacher's *kanji* (calligraphy character) to my wife and her parents. They smiled at these openings, which they immediately called *suki Ma*.

When I compared my Ma character to my teacher's Ma character, mine was basic, bumpy, cramped. It lacked strength and discipline. One gate was a bit firm and thick, while the other was more fragile, and thinner.

For my Ma character, the gates and the sun didn't have any gaps inside. They were completely closed. As I thought about it more, I realized that it mirrored how I viewed life at that time. Things should be finalized, with no cracks in it. In life, an opening in some situations means we are exposed, we will be criticized for not completing the work. It suggests that we haven't done our job properly that our work has flaws and it must be corrected and finished off.

Looking at my teacher's drawing, the gates looked like two people coexisting in a shared space and the *hi* (sun) character represented opportunity that wasn't completely set in stone. There were still possibilities. My own Ma showed that these gates, these people, might be arguing, finding no common ground, sticking to their opinions. One person was thick and robust, perhaps stronger and forcing their opinion onto the other. My *hi* character in the middle meant fixed positions between the two with no room to move. When I looked at my teacher's Ma, these small gaps suggested that these two gates weren't so closed off.

Like human beings, we have all those foundations, those non-negotiables, those feelings and opinions we resist changing. Yet there will always be openings, times when we let people in, times when we are open to new ideas, times when we are ready to change our minds. A *suki Ma* encourages us not to assume a person will always stick to their opinion nor to assume that the world will always be dark. We just need to be patient and wait for the right space and time when these openings appear, when we and the world are ready to enter them again, and when the light is ready to return.

FIND YOUR LIMINAL SPACE

Suki Mas can also be termed as liminal – in-between private spaces away from public space, spaces where we can remove our company masks, where anything can happen and we aren't confined by rules, or obligations. In other words, we can talk freely and we can be ourselves. In these cracks, these spaces, we don't worry about looking perfect.

Dr Harriet Shortt from the University of the West of England conducted a 9-month study in 5 hair salons and identified these liminal in-between spaces in stairwells, corridors, toilets, even dark areas in an office. According her research, these liminal spaces have multiple functions. Employees used them to escape from the public spotlight, hide from others, suspend their work obligations, vent or gossip, de-stress, reclaim their personal space. Some used corridors to distance themselves from company politics. On a more positive note, these liminal spaces foster creativity as the participants were not constrained by politics or protocol. They could think freely. Her article suggested why we need more of these spaces for employee well-being, bonding and innovation.

BUILD YOUR OWN PRIVATE SPACE

We want to bond with our family, friends, colleagues and neighbours, be there for each other. Yet we also love our private spaces to engage in our private interests, our private thoughts. In his online presentation *MA in Contemporary Japanese Architecture* for Japan House Los Angeles, Japanese architect Manabu Chiba showed us how small openings in houses give that privacy while maintaining that connection to others.

Manabu Chiba designed a family home in Kanagawa prefecture, near Kamakura, for two parents and their two children. As a family, they wanted to feel connected but they wanted their own private space. He created openings in the rooms, by not having the walls extend all the way down to the floor. This incomplete design created those small *suki Mas* so that family members could peak into each other's rooms, while still having that privacy and distance. He also added a window between rooms so that family members could open them up when they wanted to communicate with each other, while still maintaining their own personal space.

But what if there is no physical space between us? Can we have our private space while in the same room and still feel connected – even in silence?

ADD A DASH OF SILENCE

In Japan, silence is the glue that holds families, friends and colleagues together. In their book *The Japanese Mind*, Roger Davies and Osamu Ikeno write about the concept of *Najimu* and how Japanese develop deep attachments to others, how they can still find their privacy, even while in the same room with others and not saying a single word to each other. According to Roger Davies and Osamu Ikeno, the mere physical presence of another human being at home or at work, even in silence is enough to connect us and give us that feeling of belonging.

Suki Mas are those silent periods, moments where silence creates that opening in the space between us. Silence gives us permission to focus on our own private thoughts, our own hobbies, our work, retreat into our private worlds. Silence offers us a solution for finding harmony in small shared spaces. In 2020, particularly in Japan, families had to renegotiate their spaces with others. As family members brought their work or their school home with them, space that people often had to themselves was gone. For those families who had large apartments or houses, they could go into another private room to reclaim their space. However, in homes where the space was limited, they needed to find their own private space, somewhere like going to the other end of the room, sitting in front of a table or couch that separates and connects in that silence.

If you find yourself fighting over a physical space with a friend, family member or colleague, try adding a dash of silence. Take a few steps back, pick up a book, text a friend, read an article on your phone. Try writing something privately, say nothing and enjoy that silent private space.

IMAGINE AN EXCEPTIONAL SPACE

Our *suki Mas* can be invisible but still felt. These moments are also unpredictable, random events when human beings serendipitously come across an imaginary pause, a temporary non-physical reprieve from their obligations and worries. I have discovered that saying the right words, asking the right questions to our friends, family and clients can also create those moments, open up those imaginary safe places to dream and celebrate life.

For me at least, I can say that these cracks are breakthrough moments when we are no longer leaning back with our arms crossed thinking limitations. We are leaning forward with an open mind, imagining possibilities, getting ready to make changes to our lives. I have learned that these openings are time sensitive and they can disappear as quickly as they appeared, so we need to seize these moments and opportunities that life gives us before they disappear.

I remember coaching a client about how she dealt with a noisy neighbour. My client, unable to sleep, asked her neighbour to quiet down but apparently it was not enough. It was still noisy. After a few years of enduring this noise, she moved to another apartment. This apartment was quiet, and while it was enjoyable in the beginning, the client couldn't help but wonder when that noise would come back. My client was so conditioned to that life of noise, she was waiting for that noise to return to her new home. As I listened, I told her it's hard to control the noise outside our apartment and it was possible that noise could come back – but not right now. When I said these last four words, she froze and became silent. Noticing this change, this shift in energy, I asked her to imagine how it felt to have that silence right now. As I asked this, I noticed her body language softening up, her mood becoming more positive as she spoke about that silence, her sense of relief became obvious as if some burden had been lifted.

While that stress, that work, that concern will still be waiting for us after this pause, we will at least be refreshed, ready to approach it with renewed mindset. When we imagine and dream of a temporary escape, our body softens, and positive emotions are released. Social Psychologist Barbara Fredrickson, author of *Positivity*, explains how positive emotions can counteract the impact the negative ones have on us. The positive emotions from these imaginary spaces get us ready for our return back to reality.

We can create more of these imaginary restorative spaces, by getting ourselves to imagine exceptions, times when our boss isn't shouting at us, times when there is no noise, times when life isn't as bad as it is now. While it is tempting for us to fast forward to that difficult life that waits for us after the pause, why not try something different? Describe what that space looks like, experience it as if you are physically there. Imagine that exceptional space. Hold that space. Stay in it as long as you can.

RECHARGE BETWEEN MEETINGS

A *suki ma* can be a free moment to recharge between meetings. A research study by Microsoft's Human Factors Lab found that taking breaks between meetings reduced meeting fatigue and stress levels, and enhanced productivity. In this study, 14 participants coming from either Microsoft or an external company participated in two different meeting session types. On one day, participants attended four back-to-back half-hour meetings that were all different in nature. Some meetings involved office layout design, others involved marketing planning tasks. On the other day, these meetings of the same duration and variety had 10-minute breaks between each meeting. During these breaks, participants meditated with the Headspace application.

During these meetings and the transition period between them, the participants wore electroencephalogram (EEG) equipment to monitor their brain activity of beta waves – the brain waves associated with stress. The results showed that beta wave activity (stress levels) was lower when participants had 10-minute breaks between meeting calls than when they didn't have those breaks.

The research also revealed that the transitioning periods between meetings also had high beta level activity. This is possibly because participants need to switch topics, mentally prepare themselves for what to say and do during those meetings, which makes it stressful. The results showed that taking these breaks between meetings reduced the build-up of beta waves stress by allowing the brain to rest for those 10 minutes and give a smoother transition to the next meeting. These breaks not only relieved stress, they improved performance. When beta wave levels were low, participants were more focused and engaged.

Meditation has been proven to reduce stress, but not all of us want to meditate, nor does it work for all of us. There are other ways to create those restorative pauses between meetings. Going for a walk, sitting underneath the tree at a nearby park might work. One would think that living in a big city like Tokyo, in a city filled with skyscrapers, there are no places for downtime. The fact is that Tokyo is 40% forest and there are, in fact, private park areas tucked in between its skyscrapers. Located next to Harajuku Station, you can find Yoyogi Park. This forested area is massive. It has a quiet walking path that leads to Meiji Shrine, one of the most famous shrines in Japan. The park is also an ideal place to sit on a bench or lean against a tree and enjoy lunch or to physically and mentally pause from the stresses of work. In Shinagawa, on the premises of a hotel, one can sit in a peaceful Zen garden in silence to rejuvenate, even though the busy, noisy city is 100 meters away.

CHAPTER 11: *SUKI MA* - TAKE A DEEP BREATH

DOWNTIME IN TOKYO

If you don't have the luxury of a 30-minute break then turning off the screen, doodling, doing something creative like Japanese calligraphy or just sitting inside your room in silence can reduce those stress levels. Whenever I am driving between meetings and tasks, I don't rush out of the car once I arrive at the destination, I sit in the car for a few minutes and enjoy that silence and stillness.

ADD STUDIO GHIBLI DOWNTIME

Studio Ghibli animation films are famous for their silence, their pauses, their power to transport us into a fantasy world, their ability to free us to imagine and feel young again.

Founded in 1985 by Hayao Miyazaki and Isao Takahata, Studio Ghibli has produced award-winning films, including the academy-award winning movie *Spirited Away*. Their Studio Ghibli Museum in Tokyo is a one of the top destinations for international travellers visiting Japan.

When you watch these films, you can see and feel that Ma. During these films the characters will pause, sit down, say nothing, sigh, look out into nature, even ponder where they are in their journey. In an interview with famous film critic Roger Ebert, Hayao Miyazaki mentioned that Ma has a strong presence in his films. This pause is an escape for the character and audience, a breathing space that frees them, gives them time to experience awe, joy, empathy – strong emotions that stay with the audience longer than the "non-stop action, sound and cheerfulness" he believed are typical of American films. Hayao Miyazaki added that American film makers are hesitant to use pauses and silence because they worry the audience will get bored and walk out of the theatre.

To demonstrate what Ma was, Miyazaki clapped his hands three or four times in front of Ebert, and then explained what was behind that clap:

> The time in between my clapping is Ma. If you just have non-stop action with no breathing space at all, it's just busyness, but if you take a moment, then the tension building in the film can grow into a wider dimension. If you just have constant tension at 80 degrees all the time you just get numb.

In reading this, I thought Hayao Miyazaki was suggesting that we risk becoming emotionally and spiritually numb in today's 24/7 connected world when it is difficult to take those breaks, when it is hard to create more white spaces in our lives. Today's workplace has little time for these *suki Mas*. It is more performance oriented than what it was 30 years ago when I entered the corporate world. Back then, we weren't constantly bombarded with targets and performance. We didn't have to worry about receiving death stares from managers the minute we lifted our heads up to get a glass of water, a cup of coffee or take a trip to the restroom. We didn't have to worry that our every move, every word, every email gauged how much of a performer we were. We had those spaces to stop and think, chat with colleagues, enjoy working in the office.

The world has become a superhighway and many of us want to get off for good, but for some reason we feel the need to keep going, to go faster, to do as many things as we can in our day, as if we are competing with the world. We constantly stimulate ourselves with messages on social media, relentlessly fill our diaries with appointments. We crave to lead those full busy lives, to show people we are working hard, that we are going places, that we have a valuable voice in this crowded world.

Some of us even carry this mentality with us when we travel. We cram so many tasks into our travel plans. We think that we need to see as many sights as possible because we may never visit that place again. We think if our schedules have those downtimes, if there are white spaces in our travel plans, then we are wasting our time and money, that we are missing out on something.

The minute you feel this need to fill your workday, or to cram as many sights into your travel itinerary, pause and ask yourself, how can I add more Studio Ghibili downtime? Instead of spending 5 hours on the train traveling from one tourist hotspot to another, or frantically trying to visit all those 'bucket list' places, just please stop. Look around the area you are staying in. Explore it. Spend an hour at a coffee shop. Talk to the locals there. Learn the local history. Sit and watch the local atmosphere unfold in front of you. Visit a park if there is one nearby. Be a Studio Ghibili character. Sit in that space and pause.

PAUSE BEFORE YOU CONTINUE

Like in a Studio Ghibli film, we need these rests in our journeys as well. This can be easy to say but harder to do when we are looking forward to the finish line. In your journey, pause and ask yourself why you are doing this journey. Look back and remind yourself how far have you

CHAPTER 11: *SUKI MA* - TAKE A DEEP BREATH

come. Be compassionate with yourself for having not yet finished your journey. Praise yourself for those achievements you have made, the setbacks you overcame, and the ones that still remain ahead of you. Before you move any further in life, stop and enjoy those breathing spaces, for they don't come back – ever.

SUKI MA: *PAUSING BEFORE WE CONTINUE*

CHAPTER 12:
Surrender to the pause

When you come out of the storm, you won't be the same person who walked in.
– Haruki Murakami
From *Kafka on the Shore*

Writing this book was a journey in Ma. I knew it would change me. I didn't know on what level that would be.

I wanted to write this book in 2019, but all I had were facts and concepts from journal articles, book chapters, random and disconnected thoughts, hunches around what Ma is. I wanted to write a book that brought the magic of Japan to the rest of the world. I wanted people to see how it can change our lives, enhance our well-being.

In March 2020, I thought more about Ma, how the world was in it. The world pause made me think about the pause more. I understood more why being still is difficult, why we rush to the destination, and why it's so hard to enjoy the present moment.

As I finished my first chapter, my inner voice screamed at me to hurry up, to move onto the next chapter. I told myself to have a first draft by the end of 2020. That didn't happen.

I thought about this book while running, while having dinner, while lying in bed awake at 2 o'clock in the morning. I was sprinting to a finish line, consumed with a belief that the world needed it right away. Or was it me who needed it?

As the pages filled, and the chapters took form, I became painfully aware that this book was about my struggle to pause, my need to complete things. I was always in a rush to get things ticked off my list, to achieve, to contribute to the world. This book was transforming into an obsession, a frenzied, delusional, marathon towards a narcissistic finish line.

As I continued onward, my book transformed into a mentor. It convinced me to stop more, to slow down, even stop writing when I had to. New ideas, new possibilities emerged from a lecture I attended, from a story a friend told me, a play I watched, a book I read. Every time these ideas came to me, I discovered my book was transforming into something more than I dreamed of. It was capturing the heart and the spirit of Ma that I wanted it to be when I started this journey.

This was a breakthrough for me. An incomplete book was a good thing. It meant that my journey wasn't over and I still had more new experiences waiting for me in the

CHAPTER 12: SURRENDER TO THE PAUSE

future, more things to write. I realized that I was transforming as well and will always be transforming. That excited me.

MA IS TRANSFORMATIONAL

The transformational spaces of Ma are everywhere. They exist in silence, emptiness, a train station, rituals, a tea ceremony, spaces where we let go, spaces when we let others talk rather than argue with them. It can even come from speaking a single word. We can find them in beautiful sights that make us feel small and change our view of the world. They exist in a journey like writing a book or running a marathon along an empty undulating road, suffering, doubting that we can finish it and yet we persevere. A transformational space creates new meaning. It inspires creativity. It strengthens our bonds with friends, family and neighbours. It makes us stronger, resilient and compassionate. A transformational space can change us forever.

TEA CEREMONIES TRANSFORM US

Transformational spaces have great power to change us in times of uncertainty. The tea ceremony was one of those spaces that was said to transform Japan during the Warring States period from 1468 to 1615.

This was a dark time in Japan's history. Japan was in a civil war and social upheaval. It was divided into many small states. There were dozens of lords independently ruling their lands and always fighting against each other for control over more land and more power. Hideyoshi Toyomi was one of three lords who wanted to unite the country. He thought changing the nature of the tea ceremony was one of the first steps to achieving that goal.

The tea ceremony was traditionally a space to restore order and validate status in times of peace, but during war, he wanted the tea ceremony to be used as a vehicle to achieve peace and unification. His advisor and tea ceremony master, Sen no Rikyu created a tea ceremony, a time and space where one could temporarily forget about the fighting, the violence, the suffering and focus on peace.

RITUALS TRANSFORM

Tea master Sen no Rikyu transformed the tea ceremony by creating new rituals that slowed guests down, broke their ties with the outside world. Entry into this transformative space started when guests arrived at the tea ceremony gardens. First, they sat outside in a waiting area surrounded by nature, trees, a water stream, and connected with nature. When it was time to go to the tearoom, guests walked along a roji pathway that evoked a sense of loneliness and put them deeper into that new world.

Before they could enter the tearoom, they bowed to wash their hands in a low hanging washbasin. Washing one's hands was a purification ritual that cleansed their minds and bodies of bad spirits and intent. It was also a ritual meant to humble them, before entering the new world of the tea ceremony.

There were two more rituals that guests had to do. Before entering, weapons and other symbols of status were left outside the tearoom. To get inside, everyone had to get down on their hands and knees and crawl through a small entrance called a *nigiriguchi*. Once inside the tea ceremony, hierarchy or titles didn't exist. Enemies, samurai lords could sit and coexist with each other in this shared space, become equals and surrender to something greater than themselves. Humility emerges in a tea ceremony space.

Today's tea ceremony is less dramatic yet it still has the power to transform us. A research study by Mayumi Uno at Osaka University suggests that a tea ceremony and its rituals build empathy. The nurses participating in this 2014 study were so moved by the tea ceremony host's kindness and devotion to them that it inspired them to improve their nurse–patient relationships.

The tea ceremony ritual of silence is transformative as well. There is little if any conversation in a tea ceremony and when there is talking, it is focused solely on the tea itself. Silence focuses all our senses on the event, the act of preparing the tea and host serving it to us. It locks us into this moment. Some guests say they feel a loss of self in this space, while other guests say the tea ceremony makes them confront their own mortality. Tea ceremony rituals can change us on so many different levels.

COMMUTING RITUALS MATTER

Our daily rituals, like our drive or train ride to work, are transformative. On the way to work, we slowly transform into a worker, a team member. On a train, we start thinking about what tasks and deadlines wait for us at work. We get our security card out and run it through the turnstiles, we send one final text to our friends or loved ones in the elevator and then mentally go into work mode when we walk into our office.

As we return home, we slowly transform back to being a parent, a partner, an individual. We text our friends, our families, catch up on our browsing, pick up some groceries, turn on the tv, have dinner. We need these daily rituals to provide that separation between work and life, otherwise we hold our work and home identities in the same mental and physical space, and they can sometimes end up competing with each other. We needed our commuting rituals to transition to the workplace of 2020.

One of my Tokyo acquaintances mentioned that prior to 2020 she would, without fail, grab a coffee at a café near her home on the way to work. When she started working remotely, she continued her morning coffee ritual, only this time she brought it back to her home. Continuing her morning ritual helped her shift from her private life into her work life. It transformed her home working space into a legitimate one.

RENOVATE YOUR SPACES

Rituals give meaning to our space, and so do the objects, the furniture, the pictures we have on our desk. When people moved their work from the office to their home, their new work stations seemed barren and uninviting. Sitting on a couch without a proper desk, a calendar, an office chair, made many people feel as though they weren't really working at all. We needed to renovate our workspaces, to create that feeling that we were in the office and working.

In mid-2020, many remote workers set up their workspaces on a separate floor or in a dedicated room. Others designated their workspace as a no-go space for other people during the day. Some put a partition while others purchased office chairs, new microphones and cameras for video conference meetings. While our remote working spaces never completely replaced our office space, it brought some stability. It even changed how we saw our working lives.

During this time, our home spaces transformed into a hybrid home, where our work entered the home and the boundaries between our work and home lives became blurred. We worked earlier in the morning and later into the night, our eating times changed and our private time virtually disappeared. People who had the home to themselves during the day before 2020 now had to share this private space with their children and their working partner. In this new space, families, partners had to find some way to make work and life coexist with one another and it wasn't easy.

MA IS YOUR FRIEND

Our relationships are a journey of peaks, valleys and chasms. Everything can be going well. We are living and working in harmony. Then we come across something we disagree on. An ideological gap of Ma forms, divides us and creates a space of tension. In the book *Ma Theory and the Creative Management of Innovation*, Mitsuru Kodama says that differences in opinion can create a Mental Ma, a gap of tension between our ideologies or views. It creates bad Ma.

When the Ma is bad, we feel stifled, controlled, hesitant to express our views. We worry we will be challenged, even humiliated by others, or even lose our jobs if we speak our mind. Bad Ma can trick us, make us think there is nothing good to be gained from talking and debating, that it only leads to more division and anger. It must be avoided at all costs. Unfortunately, not saying anything creates more of a divide between us that we maintain to protect ourselves.

Bad Ma can create illusions. We worry that if we enter this divide and allow others to speak, they will take over the space, dominate it with their own views, their own narratives and we will become a prisoner of it, a supporter, or worse – an accomplice. This is our ego creating illusions to keep us safe and look smart. We need to silence it.

The space of Ma doesn't have to be a space of division. Mitsuru Kodama says if we can find a way to silence our ego, this division in Ma can ultimately transform into commonality. Our ego loses its power when we stop defending ourselves and start welcoming other ideas with empathy. When we open the space and discuss new ideas, validate and integrate them, Ma can become our friend.

EXISTENTIAL MA: WHO AM I?

Any long journey where we change our thinking and habits can have a lasting change on our identity. Those who live abroad and adapt to new cultures are likely to experience an identity shift as well. However, when they return home with a new identity, they may experience conflict with their home culture. Holding two or more cultural identities can create not just a mental Ma, but an existential one. Cross-cultural research on bicultural individuals – people who have two or more cultural identities – suggests that holding these two cultures in the same space can make one feel caught between them, forced to choose one culture over the other.

For example, a Japanese expatriate who has lived and worked overseas might be discouraged in expressing their other identity when in the Japanese workplace. They feel pressured to conform to the Japanese way of working and communicating. Conversely, that person might feel hesitant in expressing their Japanese side with their foreign friends. This constant switching back and forth between cultures makes them feel like a chameleon, unsure of who they are.

Existential Ma can be disorienting and uncomfortable, and people will search for ways to reduce those feelings. One way is to choose one of their identities and leave the other behind. The other is to keep their cultures separate and to never let them meet in the same space. If they do, the tension returns. One of the reasons is that there is a fear that we will be forced to choose only one culture and leave the other behind. We see this in western countries where a second-generation Japanese teenager will speak only Japanese at home and then speak English outside the home with classmates, teachers and friends.

Keeping our identities separate and not entering a space of Ma can relieve this discomfort, but ultimately there comes a time when both identities do meet and remain in that space of tension. If bicultural individuals can stay in that tension long enough, they may learn to see their cultures not as conflicting with one another but rather complementing each other. The key is to search for those commonalities, something that they both share, that are aligned to that person's personality. Existential Ma is a transformative space to become someone new. In this space and time of Ma we search for ways to bridge the boundaries between our two cultures, who we once were and who we can become.

I HAVE NO SELF

One of the reasons why existential Ma is so stressful is because we are trying to hold on to a clear, single identity. Living overseas or going through any other life transition will make our identities seem foggy, unclear, even blank. What is happening is that our identity is changing again. It is reconciling our two conflicting cultural identities. The ego will resist this change because it wants a clear identity right now. Unclear identity is a threat to our ego. So how do we break the strength of this ego and its power to stop us from changing? How do we create good existential Ma between our identities?

One way to change is to dissolve our sense of self. A strong sense of self resists change out of fear we will lose our identity. We learned earlier that we are always changing in form. We are changing how we look, what we do, what we believe and who we are. So why hold onto something that isn't permanent?

Zen Buddhism believes in a non self. In other words, we are empty of a sense of identity, so we shouldn't become too attached to our identity. In times of uncertainty, we are holding onto our sense of self, the way things were. If we are too attached to it, and we can't validate our identity, we fight these feelings, and we suffer. If we can see our identity as having no permanent form, we can freely evolve into something else.

Teachers, for example, may see themselves primarily as face-to-face teachers and not online teachers. Given that many classes were not running during 2020, this face-to-face teacher identity was disturbed, and teachers were unable to validate that face-to-face teacher identity. If this person would dissolve that face-to-face teacher identity, pretend it never existed, this person is likely to change, and more readily become an online teacher. For me, 2020, when there weren't many teaching opportunities, this was a time for me to let go of my teaching self and evolve into a writing self.

Yet telling someone to let go of their identity, that it doesn't exist, doesn't work for all of us. This 'self' made us into who we are. It helped us break through transitions, like going abroad, undergoing a career transition. In times of adversity, we need our identity to remind us of what we believe in, what we stand for, and who we are.

A strong sense of self makes us resistant to change, yet when times change, we realize our attachment to our identity holds us back. Letting go of it gives us permission to form a new sense of self that can help us navigate through moments of transition and adversity. So how can we learn to let go when we want to hold on? We need to find letting go spaces.

FIND A LETTING GO SPACE

Letting go spaces are where we have no choice but to let go and surrender to the moments of change. I found one such space in a remote hot spring town, called Takeo. Located in the relatively unknown Saga prefecture, an hour away

CHAPTER 12: SURRENDER TO THE PAUSE

from Fukuoka, Takeo, according to many Japanese people, is in the middle of nowhere. For me, Takeo, this nowhere place, was the perfect place to find these letting go spaces.

Not far from Takeo Hot Springs, located on the foothills of Mount Mifuneyama is Mifuneyama Rakuten. Here, in 2019, I attended an interactive night show titled *A Forest Where Gods Live*. Produced by Team Lab, an organization that specializes in immersive digital art, this show embodies the spirit of letting go.

Set in this forest garden, the forest comes alive at night. The forest collaborates with digital technology and music to create a spectacular show that leaves you in awe. As you walk through the forest, the music, the lights, the art, the changing forest colours and patterns, all of this grabs your attention and senses. It blurs the boundaries between. You wonder what is digitally manufactured art and what is forest. As you experience this space with all your senses, you feel peace and warmth in your heart as you, the digital art, music and nature are transforming into one entity.

But this space is always changing in light, sound and feeling. When I visited, I remembered that I and the space were constantly changing in form. One moment I was feeling inspired and moved. The next moment, I was caught up in feelings of regret and melancholy and I wasn't trying to control these feelings. I was allowing them to change. The big lesson I learned from these dynamic transformational spaces is that we and the world are constantly transforming, so why bother holding onto one form? We have the potential to be anything when we let go.

SEEK AWE SPACES

An awe space can be a moment, a magnificent sight that silences us and changes our world view. It encourages us to let go of any feelings that are holding us back from enjoying life and being kind to each other. Michelle Shiota and her team at Arizona State University Department of Psychology found that awe spaces lower our sympathetic nervous system. They calm us down, humble us, connect us to something bigger than us. They help us see our place in the world and realize how little our daily concerns are.

But we don't need to climb a mountain or see an amazing waterfall to experience awe. We can find it every day if we stop and look closely. We can find it in a leaf that is just starting to change red as it readies itself for the autumn season. We can experience it when we listen to some heart wrenching music or even stumble across a work of art, or watch a polar bear flip over in the water of an aquarium. We can see it in a once-in-a-lifetime lunar eclipse that won't happen again for another 300 years, or we can see it when two ducks gracefully leave their wake in a still pond. We can even see it in our family, colleagues or friends as they master a new language or when they perform an amazing feat in gymnastics or any other sporting event. These days, I stop more to enjoy these awe spaces and discover just how beautiful the world is, how amazing people can be and how simple things we take for granted can move us and inspire us.

TRAIN STATIONS INSPIRE US

Can train stations be awe inspiring? We pass through them on our way to work, on our way home, on our way to play. Sadly, we forget to pay attention to these stations and miss out being inspired by them. After all, train stations can appear unfriendly, uninviting and cold. The concrete floors, the lack of natural light, the steady stream of rushing commuters – all of this hurries us to the platform and to board the next train. It's hard to be inspired by a train station when we would rather be somewhere else.

In December 2021, I visited Takanawa Gateway station in Tokyo, a new station built on the Yamanote line – the first in 50 years. I came here believing I would learn something, get some fresh ideas on how to finish my book. I left feeling inspired.

When I stepped off the train, I immediately noticed the wooden tile platform. The platform benches were also made out of wood. It was a nice change from the concrete platforms most Tokyo train stations have. This station seemed inviting. It encouraged me to explore, to stay here longer that I had planned, to ponder what the architects, builders and engineers and construction crew wanted this station to represent.

I slowly walked up to the concourse, curiously examining the steel framework supporting the building, the wooden walls, furnishings and floor tiles – all made from trees from the 2011 Tsunami-affected Tohoku region. I looked up to the great void between the concourse and the ceiling, silently enjoying the sunlight entering through the gaps in the origami-shaped roof, which allowed natural light to bathe the station. Seeing Tokyo on each side of this station, having the generous natural light pour in through the roof and the windows running along the station, made me feel part of Tokyo. It filled me optimism and gratitude to be alive.

Takanawa Gateway was intended to be a place where people from all over the world could meet, where a new city would be built around it, where people could experience the charm and transformational powers of Japanese space. The more I walked around it, stopped, examined and pondered, the more I realized this station was exactly what architect Kengo Kuma and his company had intended.

Train stations are living, constantly changing entities that bridge the past dreams of architects with passengers in the present, transforming how we view time, space and life. Takanawa Gateway reminds us that wherever we are, whatever is in the space around us, however short a time we occupy that space, new worlds open up when we pause and aren't worried about catching the next train.

ONE HUNDRED SILENCES, ONE WORD

Viktor Frankl, an Austrian neurologist, psychologist and holocaust survivor once said:

> Between stimulus and response there is a space. In that space is our power to choose our response. In our response lies our growth and our freedom.

Transformation can happen when we want to run but stay still, when we want to fight but lean in, when we want to speak but remain silent. In this space, we surrender to that moment and wait for the right word to arrive.

A few years ago, I remember being asked to coach a client on delivering a presentation to his senior management team. I jumped at the chance. Presentation coaching is one of my passions. I have been doing it for over 28 years in universities, and in companies. The thought of helping clients polish their wording, their visuals, their presentation pace, adding impact – all of this gives me a rush. At times it almost feels addictive.

In our first session, we restructured the presentation, added better words, included new pretty visuals, improved the flow. My client was energized. The revised presentation was looking more beautiful. During our final session, I sensed a shift. My client politely listened to my ideas, but I felt they weren't going to be used in the presentation. He was quite senior and I believed he felt that including all the ideas from someone who wasn't in his field wasn't a good idea. It seemed like we were caught in a polite power struggle – wanting to tell the other person what to do, but never speaking it, yet hoping we would both figure it out.

When he ran through his full presentation, he presented a visual which didn't seem great I thought. I wanted to tell him that he needed to select another one, perhaps the one I suggested earlier. I waited for a few seconds, giving myself time to rethink whether I should say anything. A few seconds later, that urge to interrupt was gone and I was 100% focused on his presentation. Midway through the presentation, he stopped, looked back at me as if expecting me to tell him what to do.

I had no words to say, other than the word, "Continue."

A few minutes later, he figured out for himself that his presentation needed some fine tuning, that some of his visuals, which he thought were perfect at the time, were no longer appropriate.

Giving my own opinion a few minutes before, while he was in a zone, would have disrupted his flow. Saying something at that time wasn't for the sake of him I thought, but rather for reassuring myself that I was making something happen, that I was saying something inspirational, that I was adding value to the conversation, that I was justifying the amount of money my client was paying me to coach him.

Transformation happens when we suspend our judgments, put the brakes on uttering the words we think are the right ones. When we pause and hold onto those words, we discover those words aren't the right ones. There may

CHAPTER 12: SURRENDER TO THE PAUSE

only be one, and that right word is still forming, gaining form and strength, traveling through this silence between us, getting ready to meet us at the end of the pause.

Japanese culture has a saying, *hyaku moku ichi gen*, which means one hundred silences, one word. When a person who has remained silent suddenly speaks, says only a few words, their word carries more weight, much more than people who prefer to talk more. I like to think that one word coming out of silence is a restraint, a time to surrender to someone else's voice, without the fear of losing our own – a pivotal moment between wanting to say something and saying nothing.

When we hold the first words that cross our minds, these words travel through those 100 pauses of silence. The words we thought of using before we paused are now being polished and refined, the unnecessary words are being left behind – leaving only the words that are needed, perhaps even just one.

In one hundred pauses of silence, our judgments and fear subside and transform into something better. In a pause, the word *fear* changes into *liberation*, *adversity* changes to *resilience*, *enemy* changes to *friend*, *fight* changes to *embrace*. One word creates a new way of living, improves our relationships, gives new meaning to our work and lives. It graciously gives us a better and more refined ending to our story.

If there is one important lesson we can take from this pause, it's the value of speaking less or saying nothing. The next time we have the urge to say something, breathe in and insert 100 silences. We may discover that the truth of our lives may not come from the many words we thought of before we paused but rather the one word that emerged at the end of it.

一百言默

100 PAUSES OF SILENCE, ONE WORD WRITING

CHAPTER 13:
Who am I becoming?

The space in which we live should be for the person we are becoming now. Not for the person we were in the past.
– Marie Kondō
Author of *The Life-Changing Magic of Tidying Up*

July 18, 2021. It is the final day of the Nagoya sumo basho tournament. Mongolian sumo wrestlers Hakuho and Teronofuji are preparing for their showdown. The winner would become the Nagoya basho champion of 2021. They are deadlocked at 14 wins and 0 losses. The last time two sumo wrestlers entered the final day undefeated was in 2012, with Hakuho being one of them.

Teronofuji, an Ozeki, the second highest sumo rank, and winner of the last two sumo basho championships is fighting from the west side. Yokozuna wrestler Hakuho, winner of a staggering 44 championships, the most in history, stoically stares down Teronofuji from the east side of the sumo ring. The 36-year-old Hakuho senses this moment. He has missed the last 6 consecutive championships but today he has a chance to return to glory, to prove to his critics that this isn't the final chapter of his great sumo career, that he still has more championships in him.

Teronofuji worked hard to get here. He was once an Ozeki but then fell down the ranks due to injury over the years. In the last year, he worked his way back up the ranks, reaching Ozeki just a few months ago. He has a chance to become a Yokozuna after this tournament with his 14 wins and 2 consecutive basho victories, 1 as an Ozeki in May 2021. If he wins today, he can be promoted to the highest sumo rank of Yokozuna, joining Hakuho at the top of the sumo mountain. According to sumo rules, 2 consecutive tournament wins as an Ozeki would guarantee that.

The sumo referee, the *gyoji*, adorned in a purple and gold robe, commands these two great warriors to place their hands on the *dohyō* sand. Teronofuji crouches down. He gives a steely-eyed stare at perhaps the greatest sumo wrestler in history. Teronofuji gets up, backs away from the center of the ring. Hakuho returns the gaze but with a more Zen-like look, yet he knows how important this match is. Teronofuji, I am sure, thinks the same as well. You can see it in their eyes.

Hakuho and Teronofuji dig their feet into the sacred dirt, kick their feet around, move them from side to side. Teronofuji crouches down and settles into his starting position. Hakuho takes a few more seconds before assuming his own starting position. With their hands and feet both firmly planted in the ground, they lock eyes on each other.

But the moment of battle has not yet arrived. Still one more ritual to perform. They both slowly get up from their positions, bring their arms to their bodies to pump their fists. They turn and hurry over to the end of the ring to towel off their sweaty bodies. Hakuho makes a menacing muscle pose to the audience, grunts, turns inward and then back towards the ring. Both wrestlers pick up salt and toss it into the air, an act to keep the sumo ring pure and free from evil spirits and misfortune. Both wrestlers slap their large bellies a few times with their hands, striking them like drummers. Their thumping, drum-like sounds echo across the ring, a signal to everyone that a great battle is about to begin. The *gyoji* sharply says to both wrestlers, 'Matanash', which means no more waiting. It is time to fight.

Both wrestlers remain upright and take another look at each other. The *gyoji* commands them to place their hands on the ground to get ready. They pause and remain standing for a few seconds. They stare at each other again. The audience claps, perhaps a sign of appreciation. They know this match is about to become famous in sumo history. The applause fades. Both wrestlers lower their bodies to settle into their final positions. Still, neither one has put their hands on the ground. There is silence. There is tension, nervous and exciting tension, the kind you feel when you want something to finish and yet you want this moment to last forever and that both wrestlers would remain undefeated.

Both wrestlers put their hands on the ground for the *tachiai*, which means rising from a crouch or the initial charge. Within a second, they charge at each other, hitting each other with gargantuan force. Hakuho uncharacteristically swings his arms at Teronofuji, slapping him. Teronofuji swings back at Hakuho. They are like two warriors fighting to the death, using any means to win. They grapple each other and cling to each other's bodies. Hakuho tries to throw Teronofuji to the side but fails. Teronofuji regains his balance. Hakuho tries to throw him to his side again. Teronofuji falls to the ground. The crowd roars. Hakuho roars like a lion and pumps his fist upward to claim victory. It is a rare display of emotion for a sumo wrestler, especially for a *Yokozuna*. But this was a rare moment, where matches such as these become written in sumo folklore.

Sporting competitions are the epitome of becoming. We don't know what will happen, who will win. We feel nervous tension. We want this anxiety to end and for the winner to be decided. At the same time, we want to stay in this in-between moment, for there is more drama to unfold. It is these moments of becoming that are longer, more exciting than the moment when we actually become.

CHAPTER 13: WHO AM I BECOMING?

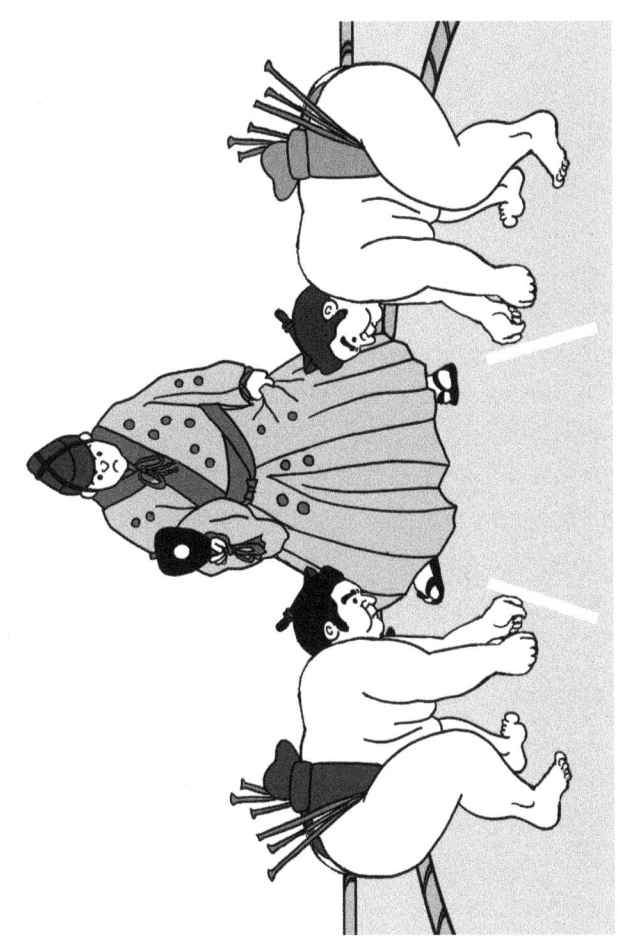

TACHIAI: A SUMO BECOMING SPACE

BECOMING SPACES: THRESHOLDS OF POTENTIAL

A becoming space is the space and time between *wanting* to *become* something and to become that something. It is an awareness that we or the situation are evolving, that we are moving towards a new state of being. A becoming space is exciting. We see glimpses of the future. We see who we and the world are about to become or can become. A becoming space awakens a faith that we will eventually get to that shore, even though we see nothing but empty sea or mountainous waves that seem impossible to pass. It keeps us going. It encourages us to keep moving towards that finish line, even though it is still hidden behind the horizon. A becoming space of Ma is a rite of passage that we must cross before we can become.

A becoming space means multiple possibilities. We can still change our mindset, even our mood. We can enter a space feeling sad, disconnected from others one minute, but when we enter a becoming space, when we pause, try new things, we sense our feelings are changing. We are feeling happier, more connected to the space and the people around it. A becoming space makes us feel alive.

In his book *On Becoming*, psychologist Carl Rogers mentioned that clients came to him in the hopes to become a better person, to become healed. Over time, they realized that their interventions with him were actually a journey of becoming. A journey of becoming is where we learn new things, push our limits. It is where we fail, where we

CHAPTER 13: WHO AM I BECOMING?

get back up, where we challenge our world, conquer our demons and make peace with our past.

For people to become a professional like an astronaut, police officer or firefighter, nurse or doctor, they must all undergo rigorous training programs. Not all of them achieve that goal. Some are stopped midway because they are unable to pass the tests. Some quit because it is too hard or they don't believe they can make it. Others quit because they realize this career isn't for them. Becoming is a chance to add more to our story, or change it. It gives us time to decide what our dreams really are, make adjustments so that we can make our dreams come true.

To become means we are a finished product, our journey is over. We have no need to improve ourselves. A becoming space, on the other hand, has no boundaries and no limitations. It allows us to pause and understand what we are becoming and the knowledge that we are still free to become whomever we want to be. Without boundaries, without end points, there is still plenty of potential left.

BECOMING IS BEAUTIFUL

To become is to be human. When we are young, we dream to become rich, to become an astronaut, an athlete, a doctor, a lawyer, a teacher, a chef (to name a few). We strive to achieve those ideal states of being. We want to become happier, to be more motivated, to be more driven and kinder. Our need to become awakens when we feel something is missing. We try to fill that void. We strive for happiness when we are sad. We want our suffering to be replaced by healing and freedom.

A goal to become gives us meaning in what we do, especially in times of struggle. It explains why we push our boundaries, why we study so hard, why we endure the hard times. During the *Great Pause*, many of us were pausing, engaging in self-discovery, searching to become something else, to prove we grew and became something during this time.

Unfortunately, we can get so fixated on our goal to become that we forget about the journey of becoming. We create illusions that the end is near, illusions that rush us prematurely to that finish line sooner than the natural flow of time. When we rush to become, we may miss the struggles and challenges that are necessary rites of passage, things that make the accomplishment worth it. Going through these struggles makes that trophy shine brighter. It brings a smile to our face when we think of the pain and struggle, the growth and learning that make up that medal every time we look at it. A journey without struggle, without blood, sweat and tears, takes the shine out of that medal.

STOP LIVING THE TIME-LAPSE LIFE

It was a cold November morning in 2020. I stood at the front of my hotel that was nestled along the foothills of Inasa mountain, overlooking Nagasaki Bay. I set my camera to time-lapse and rested it on the railing, then

CHAPTER 13: WHO AM I BECOMING?

I turned my attention to the coming sunrise, standing there for 1 hour, waiting in the cold, longing for that sunrise to come. The sky was dark, but a light blue crack began slowly forming above the distant mountains across the bay. Slowly that blue crack transformed into orange. It expanded, opened up the brightening sky. Darkness slowly faded away as the sun crawled out from behind the Nagasaki mountains and its rays slowly climbed over them. The rays moved down the mountains, crept over Nagasaki Bay towards our hotel, almost as if they were seeking me out. Buildings became brighter, bigger, warmer, more inviting over the next hour. It was becoming day in Nagasaki.

When I looked at the time-lapse photo later, I was awed by the rapid changes of the world. The sun swiftly climbed out from behind the mountains, raced across the bay. Boats that I didn't notice before sped through Nagasaki Bay. Buildings and landscape quickly changed in colour and form as the sun rose. Yet this time-lapse photo didn't inspire me as I thought it would.

Time-lapse photography is a time capsule of becoming sent to us from the past. We learn that the world is always shifting in form, moving forward, becoming something. But time-lapse photography doesn't capture the spirit of becoming. It displaces us from the pure, real-time, human experience, the excitement we feel as the world is changing in its own natural time. Nor does it embody the yearning we have when the sun slowly appears.

So why would we live our lives in time-lapse mode? It's because sitting for hours, days, months and years waiting for something to happen is boring, a waste of time. Living our lives in time-lapse mode means we can reach our arrival sooner rather than later. A slow changing space creates the illusion that the world isn't moving.

Not all spaces are that dynamic. Many spaces change slowly, subtly, so much that it is difficult to notice them if we aren't standing still and closely paying attention to these changes. What if we learnt to be more mindful, to sense those slow, fleeting micro movements, that are almost imperceptible?

UTSUROI: A SENSOR OF BECOMING

Tuning into that state of becoming means paying attention to the changes we often take for granted. We notice the energy surrounding the changes within us, the buildings around us. It exudes an energy that lures us in to that moment, wanting to know more.

In her presentation *Designing Mindfulness*, Dr. Yoko Kawai defines *utsuroi* as the gradual inevitable change of nature in the space. It is the passage of one state to another, changes we see in light and temperature when it becomes midday. Utsuroi was once thought to be the moment a *kami* or spirit entered an empty space or object. Architect Kengo Kuma suggests that an appearance of a shadow and its movement signifies the entrance of a spirit. In his journal article *Intervals (Ma) in Space and*

CHAPTER 13: WHO AM I BECOMING?

Time, Associate Professor Emeritus of Religion, Richard Pilgrim cited Japanese architect Arata Isozaki as saying that:

> Ma is the way of sensing the moment of movement. It is the expectant stillness of the moment and attending to this kind of change.

We can see these changes in nature when a leaf has just fallen off a tree to signify the beginning of the end of autumn and that winter is coming. We see it when a shadow forms and moves across a room to show the day passing by. *Utsuroi* is like a sensor for change and becoming. Our heart may notice these changes, even if we aren't aware of it. *Utsuroi* keeps us in the here and now. It senses how our mood and thoughts and ideas about life may be changing and we and things are becoming.

If you want to learn the power of becoming, I suggest sitting inside a room for a few hours to observe the changes. The natural light will change. The atmosphere will change. Walls transform in colour and brightness. A room seems bigger when there is light. Your mood may change. You may become brighter, happier, when the sun enters the room, or sombre and more relaxed when shadows and darkness move across the room at the end of the day.

WHO AM I BECOMING?

As we become more sensitive to the changes in the world, we become more aware of the changes happening within us. We discover we are becoming someone else but we may not know yet who that person is. We may need to stop and ask ourselves who we are becoming.

Spend some time and ask yourself:
1. What changes have I noticed in myself?
2. How do I handle moments of tension with others?
3. What does silence mean to me now?
4. Do I open the space and listen more to others?
5. Am I reading the air better?
6. Am I free of judgments in silence?
7. What are my relationships evolving into?
8. Who am I becoming?

As we ask ourselves these questions and get answers, we may discover we are becoming stronger, more resilient in a pause, in a long wait, in a long journey. We feel calmer when waiting at a traffic light. We can now easily hold a meditative pose. We enjoy the process rather than the outcome. In our personal and working lives, opponents are becoming advocates, enemies are becoming friends. We are becoming who we always wanted to be. Perhaps even more.

DO I LIKE WHO I AM BECOMING?

Becoming someone else can be inspiring. It encourages us to keep doing what we are doing. People who were working remotely had more time for themselves and their family. They realized there was more to life than working in an office. They were becoming more balanced, a better person, a better partner, husband, wife, partner and parent. Perhaps that is why many people these days have no desire to return to the office, or least not fulltime.

In our journeys we may notice that we are travelling off course, that we aren't becoming the person we set out to be but someone else, and we may not like who that person is. We discover that the person we are becoming may not align with the person we are or were. This makes us resentful, even angry that we are giving up too much of ourselves, what we believe in, who we are just to achieve that goal.

In our journey to becoming a successful entrepreneur, doctor, chef, athlete, artist, mechanic, influencer, or whatever we are aiming for, we may become obsessed with our goal so much that we take our friends and family for granted. We lose that balance between our personal lives and our work lives. For me, while working from home, the boundaries between work and my private life became blurred. I was working later than I used to do, so much I had little time for myself and others. I knew I had to stop and change something.

YOU CAN STILL CHANGE COURSE

In our journeys, it is important to stop and ask ourselves, do we like who we are becoming? If not, what changes can we make? How do we become the person we want to be?

Japanese architect Shigeru Ban is well known for his innovative architecture around the world. In 2006, his firm designed the Centre Pompidou-Metz building in France for an exhibition (which was inaugurated in 2010). But it was not long after completing this project that he was disappointed by what he and his profession were becoming. His profession was working for rich and powerful people, designing and building monuments and buildings – all for the sake of power and money. The architecture community, he thought, wasn't working enough for society. He wanted the architecture community to create temporary housing for buildings destroyed by natural disaster like floods and earthquakes. This revelation strengthened his resolve to continue his humanitarian work in disaster areas that he started in the early 1990s.

In 1994, he and his team designed temporary shelters made out of reusable paper tubes for Rwandan refugees. They also provided this same type of shelter during the 1995 Kobe earthquake, specifically for a destroyed catholic church where Vietnamese refugees were staying – using paper tubes and beer crates as the foundation. This temporary shelter was intended to be used for only 3 years, but it remained there for 10 years. In 2005 that church was disassembled and donated to Taiwan, which needed a temporary church to replace the church that was damaged by an earthquake. This church has become a permanent part of Taiwan.

He continued his humanitarian work in Turkey, China and also Tohoku Japan, the site of the 2011 earthquake and tsunami. He and his team created temporary three-story housing using shipping containers in Ogawa Miyagi in a baseball field. His students helped design the furniture, creating comfortable homes that the residents say they want to stay in forever.

In building these temporary houses, Shigeru Ban wondered what is permanent and what is temporary? A building made out of concrete and steel, which we think is permanent, can become temporary if it collapses from a natural disaster or if it is abandoned or torn down by a new owner and developer. In his journey to becoming a socially responsible architect he made an important discovery. He realized, "A home made out of paper can become permanent if people love it."

When we stop and reflect who we are becoming, a revelation emerges. We discover there is still more to do, more things to learn, more chances to dream, more possibilities to consider. These becoming spaces expand our boundaries, our standards, so that we become more than the person we set out to become when we first started our journey.

SATOYAMA: A BRIDGE UNITING TWO WORLDS

The Japanese word *hashi* has many different meanings. It is a chopstick, an edge, a bridge that unites two different worlds. In the Tochigi prefecture town of Nakagawa, one can find the Nakagawa-machi Bato Hiroshige Museum, which is dedicated to 19th century artist Ando Hiroshige. This museum, designed by Kengo Kuma, also acts a bridge that connects the village of Nakagawa with the shrine and mountain called *satoyama*.

According to Kengo Kuma, *satoyama* comes from two words, *sato* means village while *yama* means mountain. But on a deeper level, *satoyama* is where village meets mountain, where human-made landscapes coexist with nature and environment. In his Japan House Los Angeles online presentation, *The World of Kengo Kuma – New Form of Encounter between Tradition and Modernity in Architecture*, Kengo Kuma said that Nakagawa was once reliant on its local resources, its mountain and forests. But over time this town became more reliant on Tokyo for its resources. This resulted in the town abandoning its own resources, its own land and its own shrine.

According to Kengo Kuma, Nakagawa-machi Bato Hiroshige Museum metaphorically reunites the forest with the village once again. This museum is the bridge that connects the mountain and village through a hole in the building. The museum uses cedar wood from the mountain behind. Rice paper was made by people from the town and stones came from the quarry of the village. When people go through this passage way, this hole towards the entrance which faces the mountain, people can see the shrine and the mountain and how it becomes one with the village once again.

As I listened to this story, it dawned on me that my void, that hole in my life, was also a bridge that appeared in my journey, an unexpected point in my life where I made peace with the pause and where my past, present and future became one.

CHAPTER 13: WHO AM I BECOMING?

The Japanese character Ma represents our journey through the void, our movement towards our goal to become. The left gate represents the start of our journey. The gap between that left gate and the sun character in the middle represents the void we cross, where we think nothing is happening, that we aren't moving towards our destination. The right gate is our arrival, the destination where we become. It extends inwards like a bridge that moves towards us but we may not see it just yet. I believe that when we cross that void and stay in it long enough, when we see the connections and not differences, when we make discoveries and embrace our fears light appears. We no longer see darkness or see an empty void. We see a bridge that is forming, strengthening, inviting us to keep moving, leading us down that path to becoming the person we set out to be.

A BRIDGE TO BECOMING

CROSSING THAT BRIDGE IN OUR OWN TIME

Becoming is exciting for us and for the people who support us. Our friends, our families or colleagues are happy we are progressing towards our goals, that we are changing and becoming a new person. Yet there are times when those supporting us may push us too fast to the end point sooner than we are ready.

A becoming space is also a restraint for us, to move slowly towards the future. When we realize we are near our destination, we may race towards that goal. When we do, we may miss things that prepare us for that arrival. It may be necessary to pause and ask ourselves whether we have all the skills, the knowledge and experience to become an engineer, a police officer, a parent, a doctor, a nurse, a parent. I can honestly say that I sometimes fall into the trap of wanting my clients to reach their goals sooner rather than later. As coaches, we want our clients to progress. We want them to fulfill their potential. But what happens when our clients, our friends our loved ones aren't progressing at the pace we expect or they expect?

Sometimes in my haste to get people into reaching their goal, I'm not figuratively crossing the bridge with them, but rather standing at the end of that bridge toe tapping, wanting them to hurry up. I end up subtly rushing them to get to the end of the bridge by leading them, giving them ideas rather than letting them discover their own path.

Coaches, mentors, psychologists or anyone wanting to help others can best support them by crossing the bridge with them, and letting that person set the pace in which we both cross that bridge.

NOT THE ARRIVAL WE DREAMED OF

Noh theatre shows that our arrivals are unpredictable – hidden behind the unexpected encounters, the revelations, the wisdoms, the new-found compassion we find in our journey. The Noh theatre play *Atsumori* tells the story of how Atsumori was slain as a 16-year-old in battle by Kumagai Naozane. As we watch Atsumori crossing the *Hashigakari*, the bridge between the world of the dead to the world of the living, we anxiously follow his journey to avenge himself.

As the play progresses, Atsumori learns that Kumagai Naozane is plagued with feelings of guilt over killing him. We learn that Naozane has achieved salvation by changing his name to Rensei and becoming a priest.

ATSUMORI

When Atsumori learns that his enemy has become a man of peace and has changed his name to Rensei, he decides not to kill him. He lays his sword down to the floor.

CHAPTER 13: WHO AM I BECOMING?

ATSUMORI'S DESIRE FOR REVENGE

It is human nature to begin a long journey with preconceptions about that what our arrival will look like. We think that when we arrive, we will be enlightened, become a better person, or even feel vindicated.

ATSUMORI'S FORGIVENESS

Michiyuki reminds us that, like in a good play, our stories are filled with hidden subplots, changes in our script, changes to the story we couldn't have imagined when we first departed. In our journeys we now face the real struggles we may have expected but underestimated. In our journeys, we change. Other people change. The world changes. The person we have become at our arrival is not the same person who departed. The arrival we imagined from the beginning is not the one we arrive to. When the actual moment comes, we may show forgiveness to our enemies, even though we planned on carrying out revenge.

It is tempting to make that dream a mirror image of our arrival. Yet if we stick to that vision we saw from the beginning, we can't course correct, we can't make that arrival better, we can't make it accommodate the person we are becoming. When I coach people, I do envision their arrival, but because it is their journey and there are so many uncontrollable factors, their final arrival isn't set. I encourage my clients to be more flexible, to give them the space to pause and discover for themselves that because they have changed, they are a new person, so their actual arrival will always be different.

When I first thought about writing this book, I had dreams, visions of what this book would look like, but as I took this journey, surrendered to the unexpected sources of inspiration from people, books, dogs and even a sake bottle, the final arrival was looking different and better.

OUR ARRIVAL TIMES DIFFER

It was late March 2021 and the cherry blossom season was coming soon. I looked to my cherry blossom tree. One or two blossoms at the base of the tree had already bloomed. As for the rest of this tree, most of the buds were still inside, ready to burst out into the world. As I was doing the laundry, I looked across and saw a cherry blossom tree on the other side of the road. Many of its flowers had already bloomed. Why was that cherry blossom tree blooming sooner than mine? They seemed to be same. Was it because that tree was a bit different or it got more sunlight?

Cherry blossoms are lot like human beings. They flourish and bloom in their own time and yet we like to compare. We get upset, frustrated because we aren't developing at the same rate. We want to be at the same pace. The cherry blossom tree embraces all aspects of life, the new, current, the end. It unites them to create a masterpiece, a microcosm of life. The time these flowers emerge from their buds is the in-between stage from starting, to growing and then blossoming. Yet many of us want to see the full bloom. We want the rewards, the achievements right away. We want to achieve our potential, to heal from an illness, to find new meaning in our lives right away. Ma kindly points out to us that we blossom at different times. It reminds us to enjoy the moments when are beginning to blossom, when we are still growing.

Enjoy that moment you are becoming that flower. Resist comparing. Blossom at your own pace.

PART IV:
Pausing at our arrival

CHAPTER 14:
Susumu – move forward

*In Japanese calligraphy, the brush always goes forward
and never back, even if you make a mistake,
for the past is the past and can't be erased.*
– Japanese calligraphy proverb

On December 10, 2020, one Japanese word inspired this chapter. Not a spoken word but a written word, mysterious, appealing, and waiting for me in a calligraphy lesson in Kurume, a city in southern Fukuoka prefecture.

As I entered the teacher's old style Japanese home, I immediately noticed from the smell of cedar wood how warm and inviting it was, how it was filled with calligraphy art, all proudly displayed on the high Japanese cedar walls. One of them grabbed my attention.

I turned to my teacher and commented, "This character is so beautiful."

She beamed with pride, "Thank you. My son drew this."

"What does it mean?"

My calligraphy teacher glowed as she answered, "*Susumu*". She paused before adding, "Move forward".

I learned a few days later how moving forward is an important rule of calligraphy. In Japanese calligraphy, one must remember that the brush always goes forward and never back, even if you make a mistake, for the past is the past and can't be erased. In calligraphy, we must surrender to our brush, let it decide where it is going, let it decide how much pressure it puts on the paper, and when it should ease up. The brush decides when the journey starts, when it ends and how it ends.

SUSUMU KANJI: *MOVE FORWARD*

CHAPTER 14: *SUSUMU* - MOVE FORWARD

***

In September 2021, as I was drawing closer to this book's completion, the Mount Fuji World Heritage Center called out to me. Located in Fujinomiya on the Shizuoka side of Mount Fuji, this museum had a place in my book – I knew it. In this place, the final pages of my book were there waiting for me to discover them. In December 2021, I made a second trip out of Kyushu Island to Tokyo and Fujinomiya, to find those final pages.

The Mount Fuji World Heritage Center is awe inspiring the minute you walk through a red *tori* gate and catch your first glimpse of this building. This building, designed by Shigeru Ban Architects, is shaped as an inverted cone, and when you look in the reflection pool in front of it, it's reflected shape looks like Mount Fuji. That water in that pool comes from Mount Fuji. The building uses stream water from the mountain and harnesses it as an air conditioning heat source. This water is then redirected to the reflection pool, which according to Shigeru Ban Architects is meant to symbolize the cycle of water on Mount Fuji.

Inside the building, a 193-meter spiral slope leads gradually from the first floor to the fifth. As I walked up this curving slope, to my right were videos of Fuji from Suruga Bay, which changed every few seconds or so, revealing the different weather and seasons of Mount Fuji. Further up, the videos transformed into a forest, filled only with the occasional fox or deer hurrying through the trees, or a solitary climber calmly trekking through the forest – all in the forms of shadows. Soon the scene switched to empty rocky trails and then transformed into rapidly moving clouds and thick mist, all circling around. These scenes were shedding the worries from my mind, leaving me free to climb up Mount Fuji, at least virtually.

When I reached the final floor, I stared at the real Mount Fuji almost in a hypnotic state. Its peak covered with snow, and streaks of snow on the Shizuoka face of the mountain, made it seem like a perfectly crafted painting. The real thing couldn't be this beautiful I thought.

The Mount Fuji World Heritage Center was, at least for me, my metaphor for moving forward. The water flowing from Mount Fuji, me ascending the spiral slope and seeing the snow flowing down the mountain peak, all of this convinced me I was finally moving forward with my life, my book and, possibly, the world might also be moving forward.

BE STILL OR MOVE FORWARD?

It's safe to say that not everyone moves forward so easily. We want to but we are unsure whether we should. Moving forward evokes excitement. It also arouses second thoughts. As we move closer to that new life, our optimism about that new life ahead suddenly yields to doubt as our ghosts of the past, which we thought we'd left behind, suddenly catch up with us. They make us doubt whether we really can change, that we become someone better, that we really

CHAPTER 14: *SUSUMU* - MOVE FORWARD

can have a better life. We wonder whether we should go back, maybe because that life is all we know.

MOVE FORWARD OR GO BACK

Some of us prefer to stay where we are because we are okay with this life. Some of us stand still because we feel guilty for moving on while others can't. The people we lost, the life that we left behind, the people who are unable to move forward – all of this can make anyone hesitate to move on. We hesitate to move forward because we worry what that new life will look like. We wonder whether we are worthy of it.

In writing this chapter and having experienced my own personal epiphanies, it became clearer to me that it's easy to tell someone and ourselves to move forward, but more difficult to do. Moving forward in all its glory, in all its poetic appeal and necessity, is also a daunting, even scary, threshold we don't want to cross but need to cross.

It's hard to stay in a pause forever. We are human beings and moving forward is as instinctive as is breathing and eating. We need movement to survive and grow. If we stay still, opportunities and life pass us by. We lose the chance to heal, to transform, to become better.

NO UNIVERSAL SCRIPT

There is no universal script on how and when to move forward, nor one that tells us when we should end a moment of silence or when we should finish a book. There is no script on how to finish a work of art when there is no paint left in our paint brush nor one on how to move forward from a global pause.

Since writing this book, I have discovered that moving forward is often preceded by a pause and the act of letting go. A final pause gives us time to sit back and wait before we act, time to stop and ask someone for advice, time to find someone who will listen to our fears and gently nudge us forward. In this pause, we understand our fears of moving forward and our guilt for moving on. We stop and listen to our heart and let it decide when we are ready, and how long our pause should last. Then, without thinking about it, something inside us summons up our courage to let go and press PLAY once again.

PAUSE BEFORE MOVING FORWARD

MOVE FORWARD LIKE A SHADOW

On December 11, 2021, I came to Asakusa, an enchanting district in Taitō Tokyo that preserves some of Japan's oldest culture from the Edo era. People from all over Japan and the world come here for the shopping on Nakamise shopping street, the Buddhist temple Sensō-ji and Kaminarimon (thunder gate). I came here to see these cultural landmarks, and to explore Asakusa Culture Tourist Information Centre.

Designed by Kengo Kuma, Asakusa Culture Tourist Information Centre is a 40-meter tall building, with seven single-story bungalow style houses stacked on top of one another. This stacking creates a space between the roof and the floor of the house placed above it, allowing each floor to have a triangular shaped roof. This allows shadows to form and move, transforming the look and feel of that building and allowing a spirit to enter it. If you stay in this building long enough, you can feel the energy of those spirits filling the space around you.

While having lunch on the 7th floor, I noticed through the window this building was casting its shadow to the right of Kaminarimon. To me it seemed this shadow was examining that gate, carefully considering whether that gate was worthy to be descended upon, occupied, and blessed with strength and fortune.

For reasons unknown to me then, I wanted to stand in that shadow. So, I took the elevator down to the first floor, purchased a few souvenirs, then leisurely crossed the street. I then looked back at the centre that was now changing in form and colour, becoming darker, more mysterious. I stood at the front of this gate, waiting patiently for that sun to move westward, for that shadow to move eastward and cover that gate – with me in it.

As I watched that shadow fill the gate, I felt my tense shoulders easing up, my erratic breathing settling down. I imagined a comforting spirit entering that gate, inviting me to follow. I walked in between that gate moving forward slowly, towards the temple in the distance.

As I look back on that day now, I realize that gate was a threshold for me, a defining moment that spoke to me, reassured me that my book was nearing its completion – yet I was in no hurry to rush towards that end.

EPILOGUE:
Yoin – the long goodbye

Whenever you set anything down as you change the position, withdraw your hand as though it were parting from a loved one.
– Japanese Tea Master Sen no Rikyu
From the book *Rikyu's Hundred Verses*

December 2021, Narita Airport. As my plane was leaving the departure gate, bound for Fukuoka, I looked out the cabin window and caught a view of the marshaller, the person responsible for guiding the planes in and out of the terminal. He was waving to our plane as we were departing the terminal. Marshallers stay in sight, bowing, waiting, until we slowly disappear from their line of sight and they slowly disappear from ours. This is what the Japanese call *yoin* – the long goodbye.

Yoin is a Japanese word for a reverberation, the slow fading hum from a bell we strike at a temple on New Year's Eve, or the soothing hum from a Japanese singing bowl we tap. Many people find this fading hum, this long good-bye, comforting.

余韻

YOIN KANJI *CHARACTER*

This long good-bye, apparently originated from Ii Naosuke, a senior shogunal advisor and tea ceremony master who lived in the mid 1800s. When his tea ceremony guests left, he would wave goodbye to them, and continue to face them until they disappeared from sight. He could then go inside, pause to fondly remember what had happened in that tea ceremony. This *yoin*, he believed, was showing ultimate respect, that he valued their time and was sad to see them leave.

This long good-bye is practiced every day in Japan. When Japanese customer service staff are done serving you, they remain standing where they are until you have walked outside the store or at least out of their view. When Japanese flight attendants serve your meal and drinks, they slowly remove their hands from the plate and drinks they have served you. Moving the hand away too quickly isn't *yoin*, but rather a rush to finish that task and move onto another customer.

We show our long good-bye every day. We do it in the slow and kind act of walking a friend or a family member to a taxi, making sure they get into that taxi. When they get into that taxi, we remain where we are. We wave good-bye as they and the taxi disappear, even though it's cold outside and we want to go back into our warm homes.

Yoin is like a song that slowly fades out, like a singer who reluctantly ends their song, someone who regrets leaving their beloved audience. *Yoin* is the slow ending of a book, the final pages, the long goodbye from the author to his readers. It's the fading out of Ma, our last few seconds of being between the start and the finish, pausing and taking a final look back at the journey we completed. In this final pause, we bask in our arrival and fondly recall what we have learned. We feel proud about who we have become.

WHAT THINGS HAVE WE LEARNED?
1. A pause of Ma is life changing.
2. Pause and appreciate your spaces. They are sacred.
3. Something is always happening in a pause.
4. Incompleteness is the pathway to perfection.
5. Hold that empty space and silence. Wait for it to fill your heart.
6. Pause and read the air, the unspoken words, the silence.
7. Create that graceful meeting as if you will never meet again.
8. Open your space for change.
9. Listen to the void. You may become friends with it.
10. Even in stillness, you are moving in heart and spirit.
11. Find your space. Breathe before you continue your journey.
12. Pause and surrender to change.
13. The journey to becoming is nicer than the arrival.
14. Pause before moving forward.
15. Look back on your completed journey. Let it fade out slowly.

ONE FINAL PAUSE

I feel sad my journey with you is over, and happy that you and I are beginning our next journeys. I also hope that someone else can pick up where I left off, continue our never-ending quest to understanding Ma and the pause, like why it deserves a place in our lives and why doing nothing is beautiful.

THE LONG GOODBYE

Extra resources

Glossary of terms

Aokigahara – Known as the Sea of Trees or more infamously known as the suicide forest. It is located at the base of Mount Fuji in Yamanashi prefecture.

Dohyō – The sumo ring where bouts are held and where sumo wrestlers wrestle.

Fuji-ko – A pilgrim or group that undertakes a spiritual pilgrimage up Mount Fuji. The Fuji-ko movement became highly popular during the Edo period (1603–1867). You can spot a Fuji-ko on Mount Fuji by their distinctive white robes and their pilgrim staff they use for climbing.

Fujiyoshida Sengen Shrine – A shrine dedicated to the Shintō goddess associated with cherry blossoms and Mount Fuji. This is the official starting point of the Yoshida Trail, the most popular trail to Mount Fuji.

Fusuma – Japanese vertical, rectangular paper or wood panels which can slide from side to side. They act as sliding doors.

Genkan – An entrance hall, a space where we are greeted by our host, where we take off our shoes before entering the home. It is a holding area between the outside world and a person's inner world.

Hashigakari – A bridge that links the dressing room where the Noh actor puts on the mask, and the stage. This bridge symbolizes the transition from the world of the dead to the world of the living.

Heya – Living quarters where sumo wrestlers practice, sleep and eat.

Hinoki – Cedar tree wood.

Irimi – The strike zone in martial arts, where we are open to attack.

JR Harajuku Station – A Tokyo station before Shinjuku station on the Yamamote line.

Kage Fumi – A game played by children where they would try to step on each other's shadow.

Kakegoe – These are shouts of encouragement from the audience at the back of a Kabuki theatre. *Kakegoe* happens when an actor freezes and strikes a *mie*.

Kami – A spirit, a god, a being that is worshipped in Japanese (Shintō) tradition.

Kyushu – The most southerly large island of Japan. Nagasaki and Fukuoka are located on this island.

Kuki Yominai (KY) – KY means you haven't read the air, or the social expectations on how to speak or behave correctly. In western society, the term KY is synonymous with reading the room. In Japan, KY isn't a favourable comment.

Maai – Meeting in the space and the optimal distance and harmony between people and objects.

Ma ga ii – A term to describe that the space we are in is good. When the space is good, we are communicating and relating well. We feel comfortable.

Ma ga warui – The space between us is bad and we are not relating, not communicating well with each other. We are out of harmony and uncomfortable.

Meiji Shrine – A Shintō shrine in Shibuya, Tokyo, which is dedicated to the spirits of Emperor Meiji and Empress Shōken. It is located next to Yoyogi Park.

Mie – A dynamic pose in Kabuki theatre where the actor freezes to express an intense feeling or an event.

Miegakure – To hide and reveal. Often used in designs of gardens and shrines to give us the illusion of distance, to arouse our imagination. They make us wonder what is hidden.

Mikansei – Incompleteness is beautiful because we are not finished and there is still potential.

Nigiriguchi – A small crawl space that tea ceremony guests would crawl through to enter a traditional tearoom. Entering through a *nigiriguchi* was meant to symbolize an act of humility.

Noh theatre – Japanese theatre that has music, dance and drama. It is one of the oldest forms of living theatre in the world, dating back to the 14th century.

Ōmukō – Meaning faraway, it refers to people who sit at the back of a Kabuki theatre who shout words of encouragement when the actor freezes.

Omote – The public side or face we show to others, people less close to us.

Onsen – Thermal, heated spa bath found all over Japan. Onsens can be part of a hotel.

Ozeki – The second highest ranking a sumo wrestler can attain.

Roji pathway – A meandering pathway of randomly spaced stones that leads guests to the tea ceremony teahouse.

Senu hima – A Noh actor stops dancing, singing and remains silent to heighten the tension of the moment.

Shōji – Sliding doors that are semi-transparent.

Shachō – A Japanese word for president or a dignified person.

Shakuhachi – A wooden Japanese flute.

Shinagawa – A major Tokyo station in the southern part of Tokyo. It is also the second last station on the Shinkansen train line before its final destination: Tokyo station.

Shimenawa – A special plaited rope that is tied to, around or across an object to show that it is sacred.

Shintai – An object or person known to have attracted a spirit to have resided within them.

Shintō – The indigenous religion of Japan. Its main belief is seeking harmony between all living and nonliving things.

Sumi – The ink used for Japanese calligraphy or drawing.

Sumi e – A term used to describe calligraphy writing.

Sandō – A long walkway, a visiting path, an approach to a Shintō shrine or Buddhist temple.

Suki Ma – An opening or crack in the Ma. In business, it means a niche market. In everyday life, it means a place to think, rest and breathe.

Tachiai – When both wrestlers place their hands on the dohyō (sumo ring). They usually hold that pose in the sand for less than second before they rise and make their first charge at each other.

Tatami floors – Straw made floors that are often found in traditional Japanese homes and teahouses.

Teppanyaki – A heated metal plate that food is cooked on. Guests are often seated in front of a teppanyaki grill where they can watch their food being cooked.

Tori gate – A large stone or wooden gate that signals that you are about to enter a sacred space. These are often located at the entrance of a Shintō shrine.

Ura – The private side or face that we only show to close friends or family.

Utsuroi – An awareness of the changes in the world, the state of becoming.

Yamabushi – Mountain worshippers who seek enlightenment by walking sacred mountains. *Yamabushi* have been in existence for over 1400 years.

Yohaku no bi – The beauty of the white space we see in calligraphy and art.

Yokozuna – The highest ranked sumo wrestler.

Yokozuna dohyō iri – A ritual performed by a *Yokozuna* sumo wrestler. It happens at a shrine before a sumo tournament and also in the sumo ring during the tournament, before the elite sumo wrestler matches begin.

Yorishiro – A space that a spirit can enter and reside in it. It can be a rock, a tree, a person and a sumo wrestling ring. It is the landing site of the spirit.

Yoshida Trail – The most popular hiking trail to the Mount Fuji summit.

Yoyogi Park – A massive park adjacent to the Shibuya district and Meji Shrine in Tokyo.

Yufuin – An onsen town located in Oita on Kyushu Island.

5th station – The main starting point for most Mount Fuji climbers. Buses drop off climbers at this point. The most popular 5th station is the one where the Yoshida Trail starts at 2305 meters above sea level.

References

CHAPTER 1: MA IS IN EVERYTHING WE DO

Graham, J. L. (1985). The influence of culture on the process of business negotiations: An exploratory study. *Journal of International Business Studies*, 16(1), 81–96.

Morioka, M. (2015). How to Create Ma – the Living Pause – in the Landscape of the Mind: The Wisdom of Noh Theatre. *International Journal for Dialogical Science*, 9(1), 81–95.

Morioka, M. (2008). Voices of the Self in the Therapeutic Chronotope: Utushi and Ma. *International Journal for Dialogical Science*, 3(1), 93-108.

Murakami, K. (2017). Dialogue as Poetic Imagination in the Way of Tea. In O. Lehmann, N. Chaudhary, A. Bastos, and E. Abbey (Eds.), *Poetry and Imagined Worlds* (pp. 255–273). Palgrave Macmillan.

Pilgrim, R. B. (1986). Intervals ('Ma') in Space and Time: Foundations for a Religio-Aesthetic Paradigm in Japan. *History of Religions*, 25(3), 255–257.

Prusinski, L. (2012). Wabi-Sabi, Mono No Aware, and Ma: Tracing Traditional Japanese Aesthetics Through Japanese History. *Studies on Asia*, Series IV, 2(1), 25–49.

Sasaki, T. (1987). A Study of the Japanese Communication Style: Some Cross-Cultural Insights into Ma. *International Christian University Academic Bulletin*. IA, Education and Research, (29), 193-211.

Wright, R. (2007). Ma, the Musubi Teien and the Living Stone. *Kawasaki Journal of Medical Welfare*, 14(1), 9-22.

CHAPTER 2: SPACE IS SACRED AND MEANINGFUL

Hall. E.T. (1982). *The Hidden Dimension*. Anchor Books.

JapanSocietyNYC. (2018, June 2). *Designing Mindfulness: Spatial Concepts in Traditional Japanese Architecture* [Video]. YouTube. https://www.youtube.com/watch? v=gcGH6rqssfs

Kay M. (Director). (2018). *Little Miss Sumo* [Film]. Walks of Life Films.

REFERENCES

Nitschke, G. (1966). *MA — The Japanese Sense of Place*. *Architectural Design.* http://www.east-asia-architecture.org/downloads/research/MA_-The_Japanese_Sense_of_Place_-_Forum.pdf

Ono, S. (1962). *Shinto: The Kami Way.* Tuttle Publishing.

Rich, M. (2018, April 6). *Women Barred From Sumo Ring, Even to Save a Man's Life.* New York Times. New York Times. https://www.nytimes.com/2018/04/05/world/asia/women-sumo-ring-japan.html

The Botanic Garden of Smith College. (2019, November 6). *Space for Well-being Japanese Spatial Concepts and Architecture by Yoko Kawai.* [Video]. YouTube. https://www.youtube.com/watch?v=W5pQXrGtPFY

Wetzel, P. J. (2004). *Keigo in Modern Japan: Polite Language from Meiji to the Present.* Hawaii Press.

Wilhoit, E.D. (2017). 'My drive is my sacred time': commuting as routine liminality, *Culture and Organization*, 23(4), 263-276.

Yamaki, H. (2017). *Discover Sumo: Stories from Yobidashi Hideo Translated by Clyde Newton.* Gendai Shokan.

CHAPTER 3: CHANGE IS AN ETERNAL DANCE

Bernardi, L., Porta, C. & Sleight, P. (2006). Cardiovascular, cerebrovascular, and respiratory changes induced by different types of music in musicians and non musicians: the importance of silence. *Heart*, (92), 445–452.

Comico Art Museum Yufuin. (n.d.). Exhibition. https://camy.oita.jp/exhibition

Film at Lincoln Center. (2022, March 26). *Ryuusuke Hamaguchi & Min Jin Lee on Drive My Car, Grief, and Silence*. [Video]. https://www.youtube.com/watch?v=BI-WwaG2PSl8

Kengo Kuma Associates. (n.d.). Comico Art Museum Yufuin. https://kkaa.co.jp/en/project/comico-art-museum-yufuin/

Koren, L. (2008). *Wabi-sabi for Artists, Designers, Poets and Philosophers*. Imperfect Publishing.

Kuma, K. (2021). *My Life as An Architect in Tokyo*. Thames & Hudson.

Shizuteru, U. (1992). The Place of Man in the Noh Play. *The Eastern Buddhist*, 25(2), 59-88.

Space Archive. *(2019, November 7). Elon Musk's Complete interview at Air Force Space Pitch Day* [Video]. YouTube. https://www.youtube.com/watch? v=lS3nIyetS4I

Ueda, S. (1995). Silence and Words in Zen Buddhism. *Diogenes*, 43(170), 1- 21.

Wright, D. (1992). Rethinking Transcendence: The Role of Language in Zen Experience. *Philosophy East and West*, 42(1), 113-138.

CHAPTER 4: MIKANSEI — INCOMPLETENESS IS BEAUTIFUL

Barton, E. (2016). Why you don't give praise in Japan. BBC Capital. Accessed 31 January 2019. http://www.bbc.com/capital/story/20160822-why you-dont-give-praise-in-japan.

Chirumbolo, A. (2002). The Relationship Between Need for Cognitive Closure and Political Orientation: The Mediating Role of Authoritarianism. *Personality and Individual Differences*, 32(4), 603–610.

Davey, H.E. (2012). *The Japanese Way of the Artist: Living the Japanese Arts & Ways, Brush Meditation, The Japanese Way of the Flower.* Stone Bridge Press.

De Mente, B.L. (1997). *The Japanese Have a Word for It: The Complete Guide to Japanese Thought and Culture.* Passport.

Djikic, M., Oatley, K., & Moldoveanu, M.C. (2013). Opening the closed mind: The effect of exposure to literature on the need for closure. *Creativity Research Journal*, 25(2), 149–154.

Gauntner, J. (2012, October 10). *Hiroshima is The Birthplace of Ginjo*. Sake World. https://sake-world.com/hiroshima-is-the-birthplace-of-ginjo/

Juniper, A. (2003). *Wabi sabi: The Japanese Art of Impermanence*. Tuttle Publishing.

Kruglanski, A. W., & Fishman, S. (2009). *The need for cognitive closure*. In M. R. Leary & R. H. Hoyle (Eds.), *Handbook of individual differences in social behavior* (pp. 343–353). The Guilford Press.

Masumoto, T. (2004). Learning to "Do Time" in Japan. A Study of US Interns in Japanese Organizations. *International Journal of Cross-Cultural Management*, 4(1), 19–37.

Nakashima, T. (2007). The Synergy of Positive and Negative Space in Japanese Calligraphy. *Journal of Kinki Welfare University*, 8(2), 113-119.

Stone, A.M. & Lammers J.C. (2012). The uncertainty room: strategies for managing uncertainty in a surgical waiting room. *The Permanente Journal*, 16(4), 27-30.

Webster, D.M. & Kruglanski, A.W. (1997). Cognitive and Social Consequences of the Need for Cognitive Closure. *European Review of Social Psychology*, 8(1), 133-173.

Wimbledon. (2020, June 22). *The Trilogy | When Edberg and Becker Headlined Wimbledon*. [Video]. YouTube. https://www.youtube.com/watch?v=I3UDVVKp-Hw

Tanahashi, K. (1990). *Brush Mind*. Parallax Press.

CHAPTER 5: EMPTINESS MEANS POSSIBILITY

Baek, J. (2008). Kitaro Nishida's Philosophy of Emptiness and Its Architectural Significance. *Journal of Architectural Education* 62(2), 37-43.

Bargh, J. (2017). *Before You Know It: The Unconscious Reasons We Do What We Do*. Touchstone.

Kaplan, S. (1995). The restorative benefits of nature: Toward an integrative framework. *Journal of Environmental Psychology*, 15(3), 169-182.

Kaplan, R. & Kaplan, S. (1989). *The Experience of Nature: A Psychological Perspective*. Cambridge University Press.

Kondo, M. (2014). *The Life-Changing Magic of Tidying Up: The Japanese Art of Decluttering and Organizing*. Ten Speed Press.

Lee, S.W., O'Doherty J.P., & Shimojo, S. (2015). Neural Computations Mediating One-Shot Learning in the Human Brain. *PLOS Biology*, 13(4), 1-36.

Matoba, J. (2002). Samuel Beckett's Busy Vacuum: Yohaku in the Late Short Plays. *Journal of Irish Studies*, 17, 101-108.

Pearson, D. G., & Craig, T. (2014). The great outdoors? Exploring the mental health benefits of natural environments. *Frontiers in Psychology*, 5, 1178.

Sudimac, S., Sale, V. & Kühn, S. (2022). How nature nurtures: Amygdala activity decreases as the result of a one-hour walk in nature. *Molecular Psychiatry*. https://doi.org/10.1038/s41380-022-01720-6

Syrek, C.J., Weigelt, O., Peifer, C. & Antoni, C.H. (2017). Zeigarnik's sleepless nights: How unfinished tasks at the end of the week impair employee sleep on the weekend through rumination, *Journal of Occupational Health Psychology*, 22(2), 225-238.

Tolle, E. (1999). *The Power of Now: A Guide to Spiritual Enlightenment*. Namaste Publishing.

TEDx. (2017, December 14). *30 seconds to mindfulness | Phil Boissiere | TEDxNaperville*. [Video]. YouTube. https://www.youtube.com/watch?v=ad7HqXEc2Sc

Yamaki, H. (2017). *Discover Sumo: Stories from Yobidashi Hideo*. Translated by Clyde Newton. Gendai Shokan.

CHAPTER 6: PAUSE AND READ THE AIR

Cohen, H. (1982). *You Can Negotiate Anything*. Bantam Books.

Ekman, P. (2009). Lie Catching and Micro Expressions. In Martin, C. (Ed.), *The Philosophy of Deception*. Oxford University.

Hall, E. T. (1959). *The Silent Language*. Garden City.

Harris, E. (2005). Silence as Sound: Handel's Sublime Pauses. *Journal of Musicology*, 22 (4): 521–558.

Komiya, N. & Tudor, K. (2016). 'Reading the air', finding common ground: reconsidering Rogers' therapeutic conditions as a framework for understanding therapy in Japan. *Asia Pacific Journal of Counselling and Psychotherapy*, 7(1-2), 26-38.

Levitt, H. M., & Morrill, Z. (2021). Measuring silence: The pausing inventory categorization system and a review of findings. In A. Dimitrijević & M. B. Buchholz (Eds.), *Silence and silencing in psychoanalysis: Cultural, clinical, and research perspectives* (pp. 233–250). Routledge/Taylor & Francis Group.

Levitt, H. M. (2001). The sounds of silence in psychotherapy: The categorization of clients' pauses. *Psychotherapy Research*, 11(3), 295-309.

Lufkin, B. (2020). *How 'reading the air' keeps Japan running.* BBC worklife. https://www.bbc.com/worklife/article/20200129-what-is-reading-the-air-in-japan

Scott, A. C. (1999). *The Kabuki Theatre of Japan.* Dove Publications.

Trompenaars, F. & Hampden-Turner, C. (1997). *Riding the Waves of Culture: Understanding Cultural Diversity in Global Business.* McGraw-Hill.

Yoshino, K. (2017). *Reading the Air: Invisible Rules That Stifle Japanese Companies.* Globis Insights. https://globisinsights.com/career-skills/communication/reading-the-air/

CHAPTER 7 MAAI: CREATE A GRACEFUL SPACE

Buckton, M. (2009). *Sumo, a sport of humble respect and grand entrances.* The Japan Times. Available at: https://www.japantimes.co.jp/sports/2009/02/20/sumo/sumo-a-sport-of-humble-respect-and-grand-entrances/#.Xrn-9WgzaUk

Davies, R. Ikeno, O. (2002). *The Japanese Mind.* Tuttle Publishing.

Dimitrijević, A. (2021). Silence as a manifestation of resistance. In A. Dimitrijević & M. B. Buchholz (Eds.), *Silence and silencing in psychoanalysis: Cultural, clinical, and research perspectives* (pp. 142–156). Routledge/Taylor & Francis Group.

Gunning, J. (2018). *Hard work pays off for good guy Tochinoshin.* The Japan Times. Available at: https://www.japantimes.co.jp/sports/2018/01/31/su mo/hard-work-pays-off-good-guy-tochinoshin/#.XroJ8WgzaUk

Kono, T. (2019). Phenomenology of Ma and Maai: An Interpretation of Zeami's Body Cosmology from a Phenomenological Point of View. *New Generation Computing*, 37, 247–261.

Masciotra, D. Ackermann, E. & Roth, W.M. (2001). "Maai": The Art of Distancing in Karate-Do Mutual Attunement in Close Encounters. *Journal of Adult Development*, 8, 119–132.

Mogi, K. (2022). *The Way of Nagomi: How to Live a Balanced and Harmonious Life the Japanese Way.* Quercus.

Suwa, M. (2019). How Could and Should "Maai", Empathetic Relation from Second-Person's Viewpoint, Be Studied? *New Generation Computing*, 37, 7–323.

Tetsuro, W. (1996). *Watsuji Tetsuro's Rinrigaku: Ethics in Japan*. State University of New York Press.

CHAPTER 8: OPEN YOUR SPACE FOR CHANGE

Das Kranzbach. (2018, September 18). *Das Kranzbach Meditation House by Kengo Kuma*. [Video]. YouTube. https://www.youtube.com/watch?v=skVINrNvpwY

DeCharms, R. (1968). *Personal causation: the internal affective determinants of behavior*. Academic Press.

DeCharms, R. (1981). Personal causation and locus of control: Two different traditions and two uncorrelated measures. In H. M. Lefcourt (Ed.), *Research with the locus of control construct. Vol. l.'Assessment methods* (pp. 337-358). Academic Press.

Fischer, R. & Ury, W. (2011). *Getting to Yes: Negotiating Agreement Without Giving In (Updated version)*. Penguin Publishing Group.

TEDx (2015). The power of listening | William Ury | *TEDxSanDiego*. [Video]. YouTube. https://www.youtube.com/watch?v=saXfavo1OQo

Omer, A. Appleby, R.S, & Little, D. (2015). *The Oxford Handbook of Religion, Conflict, and Peacebuilding*. Oxford University Press.

Ryan, R.M. & Deci E.L. (2017). *Self-determination theory: Basic psychological needs in motivation, development, and wellness.* Guilford Press.

Ryan, R.M. & Deci E.L. (2000). Self-determination theory and the facilitation of intrinsic motivation, social development, and well-being. *American Psychologist*, 55(1), 68–78.

Shockley, K. M., Gabriel, A. S., Robertson, D., Rosen, C. C., Chawla, N., Ganster, M. L., & Ezerins, M. E. (2021). The fatiguing effects of camera use in virtual meetings: A within-person field experiment. *Journal of Applied Psychology*, 106(8), 1137–1155.

Urabe T. (2017). Ma Thinking in Architectural Space, Mentality and Action: The Impact of Ma Thinking on Lifestyle Design. In M. Kodama (Ed.), *Ma Theory and the Creative Management of Innovation*, pp 215-228. Palgrave Macmillan.

Westbank Corp (2017, April 5). *Kengo Kuma's Vancouver Tea House - AlbernibyKuma - Westbank.* [Video]. YouTube. https://www.youtube.com/watch?v=FIuQQb-toi8

CHAPTER 9: BE FRIENDS WITH THE VOID

Bridges, W. (2004). *Transitions: Making Sense of Life's Changes.* Hachette Books.

Grant, A. (2021, April 19). There's a Name for the Blah You're Feeling: It's Called Languishing. New York Times. 2021. https://www.nytimes.com/2021/04/19/well/mind/covid-mental-health-languishing.html

Griffiths, J. & Mack, K. (2007). Going to Sea: Co-creating the Aesthetic Dimension of Shipboard Organizational Life, *Culture and Organization*, 13(4), 267-281.

Handa. R. (1994). Mu in Details of Japanese Contemporary Architecture: Can the Void Represent an Idea? In: A Community of Diverse Interests: *Proceedings of the 82nd Annual Meeting of the Association of Collegiate Schools of Architecture*, Montréal, Quebec. March 12-15, 1994. pp 280-285.

Hatano, A., Ogulmus, C., Shigemasu, H., & Murayama, K. (2022). Thinking about thinking: People underestimate how enjoyable and engaging just waiting is. *Journal of Experimental Psychology: General*. Advance online publication. https://doi.org/10.1037/xge0001255

Keyes, C.L.M. (2002). Selecting Outcomes for the Sociology of Mental Health: Issues of Measurement and Dimensionality. *Journal of Health and Social Behavior*, 43(2), 207-222.

Louisiana Channel. (2018, September, 11). *Hiroshi Sugimoto Interview: Between Sea and Sky.* [Video]. YouTube. https://www.youtube.com/watch?v=JWh4t67e5GM

Odawara Art Foundation (n.d.). *Enoura Observatory.* https://www.odawara-af.com/en/enoura/

Royal Academy of Arts. (2014, January 23). *Kengo Kuma.* [Video]. YouTube. https://www.youtube.com/watch?v=Ew4rx6oQOgY

Sugimoto, H. (n.d.). Seascapes. Hiroshi Sugimoto. https://www.sugimotohiroshi.com/seascapes-1

Taniguchi, S., Chang, K., Aida, A., & Suzuki, M. (2003). Research on image of healing received from garden landscape. *Journal of Agricultural Science-Tokyo Nogyo Daigaku*, 48(3): 115-127.

Tanizaki, J., Harper, T, J. & Seidensticker, E. G. (1977). *In Praise of Shadows.* Leete's Island Books.

Turner, V. (1969). *The Ritual Process: Structure and Anti-Structure.* Aldine Transaction.

Turner, V. (1967). *The Forest of Symbols: Aspects of Ndembu Ritual.* Cornell University Press.

Wilson, T. D., Reinhard, D. A., Westgate, E. C., Gilbert, D. T., Ellerbeck, N., Hahn, C., Brown, C. L., & Shaked, A. (2014). Social psychology. Just think: the challenges of the disengaged mind. *Science*, 345(6192), 75–77.

CHAPTER 10: MICHIYUKI — JOURNEY IN STILLNESS

Fredrickson, B. L. (2004). The broaden and build theory of positive emotions. *Philosophical Transactions of the Royal Society*, 359, 1367–1377.

Halford, A. & Halford, G.M. (1965). *The Kabuki Handbook: A Guide to Understanding and Appreciation.* Tuttle Publishing.

JapanSocietyNYC. (2018, June 2). *Designing Mindfulness: Spatial Concepts in Traditional Japanese Architecture* [Video]. YouTube. https://www.youtube.com/watch?v=g-cGH6rqssfs

Lucas, M. (2014). Nomadic' organization and the experience of journeying: Through liminal spaces and organizing places, *Culture and Organization*, 20(3), 196-214.

Motosugi, S. (2017). Ma in traditional Japanese theatre. The Ma of space and Ma of time. In M. Kodama (Ed.), *Ma theory and the creative management of innovation*, pp. 195-214. Palgrave MacMillan.

Udaka, M. (2010). *The Secrets of Noh Masks*. Kodansha International.

CHAPTER 11: SUKI MA — TAKE A DEEP BREATH

Cyranoski, D. (2007, August 29). *Flying insects threaten to deafen Japan*. Nature, 448, 977. https://www.nature.com/articles/448977a

Davies, R. Ikeno, O. (2002). *The Japanese Mind*. Tuttle Publishing.

Ebert, R. (2002, September 12). Hayao Miyazaki interview. Roger Ebert.com. https://www.rogerebert.com/interviews/hayao-miyazaki-interview

Japan House Los Angeles. (2021, July 29). MA in Contemporary Japanese Architecture [Video]. JAPAN HOUSE Los Angeles. https://www.japanhousela.com/events/ma-in-contemporary-japanese-architecture/

Microsoft (April 20, 2021). *Research Proves Your Brain Needs Breaks: New options help you carve out downtime between meetings*. Available at: https://www.microsoft.com/en-us/worklab/work-trend-index/brain-research

Shortt, H. (2015). Liminality, space and the importance of 'transitory dwelling places' at work. *Human Relations*, 68(4) 633–658.

CHAPTER 12: SURRENDER TO THE PAUSE

Arizona State University. (2019, June 3). *Research that takes your breath away: The impact of awe*. Arizona State University. https://news.asu.edu/20190103-research-takes-your-breath-away-impact-awe

Bennett. J. M. (2014). Cultural marginality: Identity issues in global leadership training, in J. S. Osland, M. Li, & Y. Wang (Eds.), *Advances in Global Leadership* (vol. 8, pp. 269 – 292). Emerald Group.

David, S. (2016). *Emotional Agility: Get Unstuck, Embrace Change and Thrive in Work and Life*. Penguin Life.

Greater Good Science Center. (2016, August 18). *Lani Shiota:How Awe Transforms the Body and Mind*. [Video]. YouTube. https://www.youtube.com/watch?v=u-W8h3JIMmVQ

Isozaki, A. (2006). *Japan-ness in Architecture, translated by Kohso Sabu*. MIT Press.

JAPAN HOUSE Los Angeles. (2021, April 27). *MA in Contemporary Art with teamLab* [Video]. JAPAN HOUSE Los Angeles. https://www.japanhousela.com/events/ma-in-contemporary-art/

Kanno, Y. (2000). Bilingualism and Identity: The Stories of Japanese Returnees. *International Journal of Bilingual Education and Bilingualism*, 3(1), 1–18.

Kuma, K. (2021). *My Life as An Architect in Tokyo*. Thames & Hudson.

Kengo Kuma and Associates. (n.d.). *Takanawa Gateway Station*. https://kkaa.co.jp/works/architecture/takanawa-gateway-station/

Kodama, M. (2017). Ma and Innovation Management. In M. Kodama (Ed.), *Ma theory and the creative management of innovation*, pp. 1-22. Palgrave MacMillan.

Kodama, M. & Yasuda, T. (2017). Managing Serendipity Through Ma Thinking: Lessons of the Invention and Commercialization of Blue LED (Awarded the Nobel Prize in Physics), In M. Kodama (Ed.), *Ma theory and the creative management of innovation*, pp. 81-102. Palgrave MacMillan.

Murakami, H. (2005). *Kafka on the shore*. Vintage.

NHK WORLD-JAPAN. (2021, August 26). *The Kengo Kuma Monologue: 5. Takanawa Gateway Station - NHK WORLD-JAPAN*. [Video]. https://www.youtube.com/watch? v=trxNUl5XxOY

Shiota, M. N. & Keltner, D. (2007). The nature of awe: Elicitors, appraisals, and effects on self-concept. *Cognition and Emotion*, 21 (5), 944-963.

Team Lab. (2018, August 12). *A Forest Where Gods Live*. [Video]. YouTube. https://www.youtube.com/watch? v=HbxQIQ8IxM

Uno, M. (2017). Changes in Japanese Nurses' Awareness of Patient Interactions Following a Japanese Tea Ceremony. *Open Journal of Nursing*, 7, 770–778.

West, A. L., Zhang, R., Yampolsky, M., & Sasaki, J. Y. (2017). More than the sum of its parts: A transformative theory of biculturalism. *Journal of Cross-Cultural Psychology*, 48(7), 963–990.

CHAPTER 13: WHO AM I BECOMING?

Akama, Y. (2015). Being awake to Ma: designing in between-ness as a way of becoming with. *Codesign: International Journal of CoCreation in Design and the Arts*, 11(3-4), 262-274.

Baek, J. (2013). Between Material Sensuousness and Thingness: The Significance of the Structural Glass in Kengo Kuma's Water/Glass House from the Perspective of Phenomenology. *Journal of Asian Architecture and Building Engineering*, 12(1), 1-7.

JAPAN HOUSE Los Angeles. (2021, June 23). The World of Kengo Kuma –New Form of Encounter between Tradition and Modernity in Architecture [Video]. JAPAN HOUSE Los Angeles. https://www.japanhousela.com/events/the-world-of-kengo-kuma/

JapanSocietyNYC. (2018, June 2). *Designing Mindfulness: Spatial Concepts in Traditional Japanese Architecture* [Video]. YouTube. https://www.youtube.com/watch? v=gcGH6rqssfs

Pilgrim, R. B. (1986). Intervals ('Ma') in Space and Time: Foundations for a Religio-Aesthetic Paradigm in Japan. *History of Religions*, 25(3), 255–257.

Rogers, C. (1995). *On Becoming A Person: A Therapist's View of Psychotherapy* (2nd ed. Edition). Harper One.

TED (2013, August 14). *Shigeru Ban: Emergency shelters made from paper* [Video]. YouTube. https://www.youtube.com/watch?v=q43uXdOKPD8

CHAPTER 14: SUSUMU — MOVE FORWARD

Flint-Sato, C. & Kawabe, S. (1999). *Japanese Calligraphy: The Art of Line and Space*. Kaifusha.

Kengo Kuma Associates. (n.d.). *Asakusa Culture Tourist Information Centre.* https://kkaa.co.jp/works/architecture/asakusa-culture-tourist-information-center/

Shigeru Ban Architects. (n.d.). *Mt. Fuji World Heritage Centre.* http://www.shigerubanarchitects.com/works/2017_fujisan/index.html

EPILOGUE: YOIN — THE LONG GOODBYE

Iguchi, K. (2020). *Rikyu's Hundred Verses in Japanese and English.* Tankosha.

Plutschow, H. E. (2003). *Rediscovering Rikyu and the Beginnings of the Japanese Tea Ceremony.* Global Oriental.

ABOUT THE AUTHOR:
Tom Frengos

間

Tom Frengos is an explorer, author, trainer and coach who has dedicated his life to helping people achieve their potential and live a more meaningful life.

Born in Canada, he has lived in Japan, Korea and Australia, and, in that time, he has designed and delivered training programs in the areas of cross-cultural intelligence, self-improvement, coaching, presentation and conflict resolution skills. He is currently based in Japan where he teaches coaching, cross-cultural and personal development courses that use the principles on which this book is based.

Tom holds a Masters of Applied Science in Psychology of Coaching, a Masters in Education and an Honours Bachelor of Psychology.

Milton Keynes UK
Ingram Content Group UK Ltd.
UKHW051138100924
448143UK00018B/173